Spiralizer Cookbook

Top 98 Veggie-Friendly Spiralizer Recipes

From Sweet Potato Fries and Zucchini Ribbons To Carrot Rice and Beet Noodles

Table of Contents

Introduction

I would like to thank and congratulate you for buying the book *"Spiralizer Cookbook: Top 98 Veggie-Friendly Spiralizer Recipes – From Sweet Potato Fries and Zucchini Ribbons to Carrot Rice and Beet Noodles."*

This book contains essential tips and proven techniques on spiralizing, a simple yet creative method of transforming vegetables and fruits into crisp and beautiful noodles, rice, pasta, ribbons and curls. This technique will help you create more vegetable-centric meals in a fraction of the time.

Likewise, there are 98 recipes in this book that will teach us how to make nutrient-dense meals with the aid of a spiralizer, a kitchen device that is easy to use and worth adding into your kitchen. Countless hours of slicing, dicing or chopping your veggies become a thing of the past: just mount your desired blade and ingredient in a spiralizer, turn the handle clockwise, and voila! Your vegetables turn into crisp cuts and strands that are ready to be mixed into soups, salads, pasta dishes and breakfast meals.

Moreover, this book contains basic know-how about the spiralizing process such as a step-by-step guide on using a spiralizer, a list of spiralizer-friendly vegetables and the health benefits we can expect to see in ourselves once we incorporate a healthier and paleo-friendly diet.

Thanks again for buying this book, I hope you enjoy it!

Chapter 1 Spiralizing 101: A Creative and Healthy Way to Eat

"Go vegetable heavy. Reverse the psychology of your plate

by making meat the side dish and

vegetables the main course."

Bobby Flay

Celebrity chef and restaurateur

There's more to a healthy lifestyle than just regular exercise and dieting: weight management starts from eating organic, plant-based produce that are high in vitamins, minerals, healthy fats and good carbohydrates. Fortunately, there is a new and effective way of including more vegetables and fruits into daily meals, and this method is called spiralizing.

Let us know more about this technique, including how it can positively affect our kitchen activities and overall health.

Definition of Spiralizing

Spiralizing is a method of transforming organic ingredients such as carrots, apples, cucumbers, sweet potatoes and zucchinis into ribbons, noodles, pasta or thin vegetable strips. You can even make rice out of spiralized vegetables by placing them in a food processor and chopping them into smaller bits.

This technique makes cutting vegetables easier and subsequently minimizes cooking time. However, in order to become successful at spiralizing, you will need to purchase a good kitchen device called a spiralizer that is easy to assemble, use and clean.

What is a Spiralizer?

A spiralizer is a unique kitchen device that turns zucchini into pasta, beets into rice and sweet potato into curly fries. It is a tool that you place on the kitchen counter for slicing and spiralizing vegetables and fruits. There are three types of spiralizers: handheld, vertical and horizontal. Most users find vertical and horizontal spiralizers easier to handle, but whatever type you choose, make sure to buy one from a trusted brand as you will use this device regularly.

Popular spiralizer brands include Paderno, Spiralizer®, Brieftons and Hemsley & Hemsley. Make sure to read on product descriptions and customer reviews first before you buy a heavy-duty spiralizer for the kitchen.

Depending on the type of blade, you can create ribbons, noodles, pasta, strips or even bigger slices. That is why it is important to match the type of blade with the dish that you are going to cook, and this will be discussed in the next chapter.

Benefits of Spiralizing Vegetables

More people are learning to appreciate the benefits of home-cooked meals, and for a lot of households the spiralizer helps them create clean-flavored dishes that look delectable but are actually waistline-friendly. Here are the main benefits of eating dishes that primarily consist of spiralized vegetables:

- Spiralizing helps us lose weight – spiralized vegetables contain fiber, protein, good carbs and minerals that boost metabolism and satiate the stomach. It also helps that vegetable noodles are low in calories and contain low amounts of sugar and sodium.

- Dishes look more appetizing – spiralizing creates dishes that are pleasing to the eye. Instead of the typical diced, chopped or julienned veggies, spiralizing creates sweet potato rice, pumpkin strands or thin cabbage strips. This technique enhances food presentation which subsequently increases the appetite for organic food.

- Spiralizing helps us go organic – the recipes found in the following chapters are primarily veggie-friendly but also contain small amounts of lean meat, dairy and protein. Nevertheless, these recipes help us transition to an organic lifestyle which will help us reach optimal wellness.

- Spiralizing makes special diets easier to follow – whether you are following a vegan, vegetarian, Paleo or Mediterranean diet, spiralizing helps you prepare noodles, soups, fries or vegetable strips that adhere to the strict guidelines of specialty diets.

Popular Dishes We Can Spiralize

As you will see in this book, the possibilities with spiralized vegetables are endless.

Here are some of the dishes you can make with the help of your trusted Spiralizer:

- Vegetable rice

- Soups and stews

- Salads

- Waffles

- Omelets

- One-pot meals

- Fries

- Pickled vegetables

- Spaghetti

- Kid-friendly snacks

- Noodles

- Desserts

Cooking is fun, easy and nutritious when you are inspired to get creative with your ingredients. The next chapter will show us how easy it is to make slices, noodles, rice and pasta with a Spiralizer as well as a list of plant-based produce that are spiralizer-friendly.

Chapter 2 Step-by Step Guide to Spiralize Your Veggies

"I think a great way to get kids to start eating their vegetables

is to get creative with them."

Jennette McCurdy

Actress and screenwriter

Spiralizing vegetables and fruits is an easy and enjoyable process: even kids and novice cooks can successfully spiralize a carrot, cabbage or an apple with little assistance. All it takes is to familiarize the parts of the kitchen tool and observe caution when mounting the spiralizer's blades.

How to Spiralize Your Vegetables and Fruits

Here is a step-by-step process of spiralizing organic produce. For this example, we are using a horizontal Paderno Vegetable Spiralizer which is a popular brand in the market:

Step 1: Suction the Spiralizer to the countertop and ensure that it is unmovable and steady.

Step 2: Prepare the vegetable or fruit you wish to spiralize. You may opt to peel it or leave the skin intact. Slice the edges to flatten the sides of the vegetable.

Step 3: Push one side of the vegetable on the spiralizer's blade. Make sure to center the vegetable for an even slicing.

Step 4: Push the pointy side of the device towards the other side of the vegetable. Make sure that the vegetable is secure and won't fall off while in the process of spiralizing it.

Step 5: Place a bowl underneath the blades that will catch the noodles. Turn the handle clockwise and see the noodles form.

Step 6: If you wish, trim the noodles into shorter strands with a pair of scissors. If you want to make vegetable rice, process the noodles in a blender or food processor to form small grains. You may also chop the noodles into smaller pieces by using a kitchen knife.

You can spiralize almost all types of vegetables and fruits such as sweet potatoes, beets, zucchinis, carrots, broccoli, cabbage, turnip, radish, apples and squash. Just remember to trim the edges of the produce so you can have a flat surface on each side.

Spiralizer Blade Know-How

It is essential to know which type of blade is appropriate for the dish you are going to make. Here is a quick guide on the types of blades available in a Paderno Spiralizer and the type of cuts and strands each blade delivers:

Blade A – has a straight blade that makes ribbons, chips and bigger slices of vegetables

Blade B – has large, triangle blades that produces spaghetti-like pasta or long noodles

Blade C – has smaller, triangle blades that creates thinner noodles and pasta that can be made into vegetable rice

Now that you are well-equipped with the basics of spiralizing, you can now try the recipes found in the succeeding chapters. Just remember to enjoy the experience and to always keep in mind that spiralizing will do wonders for your health and household.

Enjoy spiralizing!

Chapter 3 Carrot Recipes

Stir-Fried Herb Carrot Rice

If you are an avid rice eater who wants to cut down on carbs, this vegetable rice recipe is a great alternative: full of aroma yet friendly on the waistline.

Serves: 2

Ready in: 15 minutes

Ingredients:

2 large carrots, peeled

½ cup water

2 garlic cloves, minced

1 teaspoon dried oregano flakes

Pinch of sea salt and ground black pepper

1 tablespoon olive oil

Directions:

Place the carrot through the spiralizer while using Blade C. Once the carrots have been cut into thin noodles, place them in a food processor. Pulse 3 to 5 times until small grains are produced.

Heat the olive oil in a large skillet over medium heat. Add the garlic and sauté until light brown. Blend in the oregano and carrot rice then season with salt and pepper. Stir-fry the dish for 3 minutes.

Pour in the water and let the dish cook for another 3 minutes. Once the water has reduced, stir the carrot rice then turn off the heat. Transfer the dish onto a serving plate and serve immediately.

Paleo-Friendly Carbonara

This paleo pasta dish is a healthier version of the classic Italian carbonara. Instead of using refined pastas and cheeses, this recipe blends the clean flavors of carrot noodles, coconut milk and fresh herbs.

Serves: 3

Ready in: 1 hour

Ingredients:

8 carrots, peeled

4 tablespoons coconut milk

1 onion, chopped

4 slices bacon

2 garlic cloves, minced

½ cup green peas

2 eggs, whisked

¼ cup freshly-chopped parsley

1 teaspoon ground black pepper

½ teaspoon salt

Directions:

Using Blade C in your device, spiralize your carrots then set them aside.

Place the bacon in a pan over medium-high flame and cook until it becomes crisp. Remove the cooked bacon and transfer it to a chopping board. Chop then set aside. Retain a tablespoon of the bacon fat in the pan and discard the rest.

Place the carrot pasta, garlic and onions in the pan and cook for 8-10 minutes, making sure to stir the dish often to prevent the noodles from burning. Transfer the noodles from the pan to a serving plate.

Pour the coconut milk into the pan then add the eggs. Cook the mixture for 1 minute while constantly stirring it. Add in the salt, pepper and green peas then turn off the heat.

Slowly pour the coconut sauce on top of the carrot noodles then toss. Sprinkle the chopped bacon on top before serving.

Carrot Noodles with Honeyed Miso Tomatoes

Miso-marinated tomatoes bring succulent, sweet flavors to this light carrot bowl recipe that can be eaten as an appetizer or a low-calorie main dish.

Serves: 4

Ready in: 30 minutes

Ingredients:

3 carrots, peeled

3 cups cherry tomatoes

2 tablespoon yellow miso

¼ cup olive oil

1 tablespoon sesame oil

3 tablespoons rice vinegar

1 tablespoon minced ginger

4 green onions, chopped

2 tablespoons fresh lime juice

1 tablespoon honey

2 teaspoons lime zest

Pinch of sea salt

2 teaspoons toasted sesame seeds

Directions:

Preheat the oven to 400°F and prepare a baking sheet.

Spiralize carrots with Blade C, and then trim it into 2-inch long strands. Set this aside.

In a small bowl, mix together the miso, vinegar, olive oil, sesame oil, lime zest, honey and lime juice. Place 3 tablespoons of the dressing in a separate bowl then blend in the cherry tomatoes. Toss until the tomatoes are well-coated.

Place the tomatoes on the baking sheet, sprinkle them with salt and bake for 15 minutes. Once the tomatoes are roasted, remove them from the oven and set aside.

While the tomatoes are baking, place 5 cups of water in a medium saucepan and bring it to a boil over high-flame. Place the carrot noodles in the boiling water, lower the heat to medium then simmer for 3-5 minutes. Drain the water from the saucepan then place the carrot noodles in a salad bowl.

Add green onions, roasted tomatoes and the remaining dressing to the carrot noodles then toss. Sprinkle sesame seeds on top then serve immediately.

Vegan Carrot Rice and Lentil Stew

Place your spiralized carrots, lentils, vegetables and spices in a slow cooker and wait for it to transform into an aromatic and flavorful stew that is meat-free.

Serves: 6

Ready in: 3 hours 15 minutes

Ingredients:

1 large carrot, peeled

1 cup dry green lentils, rinsed

1 red onion, chopped

2 garlic cloves, minced

4 cups vegetable broth

1 tablespoon hot sauce

1 tablespoon tomato paste

2 cups diced tomatoes

1 cup water

4 cups vegetable broth

½ teaspoon turmeric powder

½ teaspoon ground coriander

1 teaspoon cumin

2 celery stalks, diced

¼ cup chopped cilantro

Pinch of cinnamon powder

1 tablespoon lime juice

Pinch of sea salt and ground black pepper

Directions:

Process the carrot in a spiralizer while using Blade C. Place the carrot noodles in a food processor and pulse until rice-like grains form.

Arrange the carrot rice, onions, garlic, tomatoes, tomato paste, lentils and celery stalks at the base of the slow cooker. Pour in water, broth and hot sauce then season the ingredients with salt, pepper, cinnamon, cumin, turmeric and coriander. Cover the pot then cook the stew for 3 hours.

Squeeze lime juice on the stew and stir in the cilantro before serving.

Carrot and Cornmeal Fritters

Spiralize your way into creating sweet and vitamin-enriched fritters: these are great kid-friendly snacks that won't spike up the blood sugar.

Serves: 5

Ready in: 30 minutes

Ingredients:

2 large carrots, peeled

2 eggs, whisked

1 teaspoon turmeric powder

5 scallions, chopped

2 tablespoons olive oil

1 cup corn meal

Pinch of salt and pepper

1 cup Greek yoghurt

Directions:

Use Blade C to spiralize the carrots into thin noodles. Trim the carrots to shorten the noodles into 2-3 inch strands.

Place the carrot noodles, scallions, corn meal, eggs and turmeric powder in a bowl. Season the mixture with salt and pepper.

Heat the olive oil in a large pan. Pour ¼ cup of the fritter mixture onto the pan then cook for 3 minutes. Flip it over then cook for another 2 minutes. Do the same process for the remaining fritters.

Serve the fritters with a side of Greek yoghurt for dipping.

Roasted Carrot and Coconut Crostino

Create this simple yet mesmerizing appetizer on your next family gathering: rest assured your loved ones will be clamoring for the recipe.

Serves: 6

Ready in: 30 minutes

Ingredients:

1 medium carrot, peeled

½ cup ricotta cheese

6 slices of French bread

½ cup honey

1 tablespoon coconut flakes

Pinch of salt and pepper

Directions:

Preheat the oven to 400°F then prepare a parchment-lined baking sheet.

Spiralize the carrot while using Blade C. Trim the noodles into 3-inch strands and lay them on the baking sheet. Drizzle ¼ cup maple syrup onto the noodles then season it with salt and pepper. Roast the carrot noodles for 20 minutes but make sure to flip it over after 10 minutes for an even roasting.

18 minutes into the cooking of the noodles, toast the bread slices in an oven toaster then top each slice with ricotta cheese.

Place the cooked carrot noodles on top of each bread and ricotta slice then top them off with coconut flakes and maple syrup. Serve immediately.

Spiral Carrots and Broccoli Slaw

This flavorful and creatively-made coleslaw is a perfect summer side dish to barbecued ribs or roasted chicken.

Serves: 4

Ready in: 1 hour 15 minutes

Ingredients:

2 carrots, peeled

½ cup raisins, pre-soaked and drained

1 head broccoli, stem and florets separated

¼ cup slivered almonds

1 ½ tablespoon lemon juice

1 cup Greek yoghurt

½ teaspoon garlic powder

Pinch of salt and pepper

1 tablespoon mustard

Directions:

Spiralize carrots and broccoli stem while using Blade C and set them aside.

Divide florets into small, bite-sized pieces. Place them in a salad bowl together with the spiralized carrots and broccoli stem, ½ tablespoon of lemon juice, almonds and raisins.

In a separate bowl, whisk together the yoghurt, mustard, salt, pepper, garlic powder and remaining lemon juice. Pour the dressing onto the vegetables then toss. Place the slaw in the fridge for 1 hour then serve.

Zesty Carrot, Cucumber and Chickpea Salad

Pair this fresh and crisp salad with your favorite protein such as fried tilapia or grilled steak. The lemon vinaigrette adds a spicy edge to the juicy and clean vegetable flavors.

Serves: 4

Ready in: 45 minutes

Ingredients:

1 large carrot, peeled

1 medium cucumber

1 cup cherry tomato halves

1 small red onion, thinly sliced

1 cup canned chickpeas, washed and drained

½ teaspoon cumin powder

½ teaspoon chili powder

¼ teaspoon sea salt

2 tablespoons lemon juice

¼ teaspoon ground black pepper

1 teaspoon lemon zest

1 ½ tablespoon olive oil

Directions:

Spiralize the carrot and cucumber by using the device's Blade C. Place the vegetables in a bowl then add onions, tomatoes, and chickpeas. Set this aside.

In a separate bowl, whisk together oil, lemon juice, lemon zest, salt, pepper, cumin and curry powder. Pour the dressing over the vegetables then toss them together. Place it in the fridge for at least 30 minutes then serve.

Spicy Carrot and Avocado Rice Bowl

Jalapenos and chili powder adds a fiery kick to this clean-flavored vegetable rice bowl that's full of fiber, protein and healthy oils.

Serves: 4

Ready in: 30 minutes

Ingredients:

1 large carrot, peeled

½ avocado fruit, pitted, peeled and sliced

3 teaspoons chopped jalapeno peppers

½ cup Italian sausage slices

1 tablespoon olive oil

1 tablespoon lime juice

½ teaspoon chili powder

½ cup homemade chicken broth

1 tablespoon freshly-chopped cilantro

Pinch of sea salt and ground black pepper

Directions:

Using Blade C, spiralize the carrots into long noodles. Place the noodles in a blender and pulse until small, rice-like grains are produced. Set this aside.

Heat the oil in a large pan over medium-high heat. Add the Italian sausage slices to the hot oil and brown the meat for 3 minutes. Mix in the jalapeno peppers, chili powder, lime juice, cilantro, broth and carrot rice. Cook the dish for 8 minutes with occasional stirring. Season it with salt and pepper.

Scoop the rice dish into individual bowls then top it with avocado slices. Serve immediately.

Caveman Vegetarian Rice Salad

The mixture of carrots, peppers, avocado and tomatoes make for a perfect paleo dinner that will make even our cavemen ancestors blush with delight.

Serves: 4

Ready in: 30 minutes

Ingredients:

2 large carrots, peeled

1 teaspoon chopped jalapenos

¼ cup vegetable broth

2 tablespoons roasted pumpkin seeds

2 garlic cloves, minced

2 large red bell pepper, deseeded

3 tomatoes, deseeded and chopped

½ cup chopped red onion

2 avocados, pitted, peeled and diced

3 tablespoons freshly-chopped cilantro

2 tablespoons lime juice

1 tablespoon olive oil

Directions:

Spiralize carrots while using Blade C of the device. Roughly chop the noodles until a grain-like appearance is produced. Set this aside.

In a small bowl, mix together the avocado, cilantro, tomatoes, onion and lime juice. Set this avocado salsa aside.

Roast the peppers on top of a grill pan. Remove the charred skin then chop the meat to small pieces. Set aside.

Heat the olive oil in a large pan over medium-high heat. Cook the garlic until golden brown then add in the jalapenos, salt, pepper and carrot rice. Allow the dish to cook for 3 minutes then pour in the broth. Simmer the rice for 5 minutes then turn off the heat.

Scoop the spicy rice into individual bowls then add equal portions of the avocado salsa and roasted peppers on top. Sprinkle pumpkin seeds on top then serve immediately.

Chapter 4 Zucchini Recipes

Meatball Zucchini Pasta

If you are on a strict paleo diet, this healthy version of spaghetti and meatballs will let you enjoy delicious flavors without the health issues produced by gluten or processed ingredients.

Serves: 4

Ready in: 1 hour 30 minutes

Ingredients:

2 large zucchinis

750 grams lean ground beef

¼ cup freshly-chopped oregano leaves

1 tablespoon salt

5 slices bacon, chopped

1 cup freshly-chopped basil

1 ½ cups pitted black olives

1 cup sliced button mushrooms

10 garlic cloves, minced

Pinch of sea salt and ground black pepper

Directions:

Using Blade B, spiralize your zucchinis into long pasta strands. Place the pasta in a colander then sprinkle it with salt. Leave it for 1 hour to let the excess water drip out. Rinse the pasta after 1 hour then drain completely.

While waiting for the pasta to be ready, preheat the oven to 425°F and prepare a parchment-lined baking sheet.

Place the ground beef, oregano, sea salt and pepper in a bowl then knead thoroughly. Make golf-ball sized meatballs with the beef mixture then place them on the lined baking sheet. Bake the meatballs for 15 minutes then set aside.

Once the noodles are almost drained, place the bacon in a pan over medium-high flame. Cook the bacon for 8 minutes with constant stirring. Mix in the mushrooms and garlic and sauté for another 8 minutes.

Add the zucchini noodles and olives to the pan and stir. Cook the dish for 5 minutes then add the basil leaves. Lightly toss the dish in the pan for 1 minute then turn off the heat.

Transfer the noodles to a serving platter then place the baked meatballs on top. Serve immediately.

Chicken and Zucchini Noodle Bowl

Blend zucchini noodles, chicken and coconut milk in a slow cooker and watch how the flavors and nutrients intensify and produce a delectable Asian-inspired entrée.

Serves: 4

Ready in: 4 hours 10 minutes

Ingredients:

2 zucchinis

1 cup chicken stock

1 carrot, peeled and shredded

1 cup chopped green onions

2 boneless and skinless chicken breasts, halved

1 cup coconut milk

2 tablespoons nut butter

2 teaspoons fish sauce

1 tablespoon soy sauce

1 teaspoon cayenne pepper

2 teaspoons grated ginger

1 teaspoon red pepper flakes

1 teaspoon olive oil

3 garlic cloves, crushed

Pinch of sea salt and ground black pepper

Handful of chopped cilantro

Directions:

Season the chicken breasts with salt, pepper, cayenne pepper and ginger. Lay the chicken breasts on a pan over medium-high flame then pour the olive oil on top of the protein. Lightly brown each side of the chicken for 2 minutes then set aside.

Spiralize zucchinis on your device while using Blade B. Place the zucchini noodles in a bowl, add in the shredded carrots and mix them well.

Pour in the coconut milk, chicken stock, fish sauce and soy sauce in a 4-quart slow cooker. Add in the garlic, pepper flakes, nut butter, and green onions and mix well. Place the browned chicken in the slow cooker followed by the zucchini and carrot mixture. Cover the pot then cook the dish for 4 hours on low heat.

After 4 hours, uncover the pot then transfer the dish to a serving bowl. You may shred the chicken if desired. Sprinkle chopped cilantro on top then serve.

Spicy Asian Zucchini Ribbons

Blend some chili flakes, fish sauce and sesame oil into a plate of zucchini noodles for a delectable Asian-inspired dish that will satisfy your taste buds.

Serves: 4

Ready in: 30 minutes

Ingredients:

3 large zucchinis, edges trimmed off and peeled

1 tablespoon chopped ginger

1 cup chopped scallions

¼ cup unsweetened peanut butter

1 teaspoon sea salt

1 teaspoon fish sauce

2 tablespoons soy sauce

1 tablespoon sesame oil

2 tablespoons toasted sesame seeds

½ teaspoon red pepper flakes

Directions:

Place each zucchini in a spiralizer and use Blade A to form long, ribbon-like noodles. Place the zucchini noodles in a bowl then sprinkle it with salt. Toss the noodles then let it stand in the sink for 20 minutes or until the excess water has been removed from the vegetables.

While the zucchini is sweating, get a small bowl and mix together the ginger, peanut butter, fish sauce, soy sauce and sesame oil. Set this aside.

After 20 minutes, rinse the zucchini noodles under cold running water. Place the noodles in a large bowl then pour in the prepared peanut butter dressing. Toss the ingredients until the noodles are well-coated. Sprinkle the scallions and sesame seeds on top before serving.

Zucchini and Kale Summer Salad

Turn your zucchini into lovely, crisp ribbons and drizzle it with tangy balsamic vinaigrette for an immune-boosting appetizer.

Serves: 6

Ready in: 45 minutes

Ingredients:

2 zucchinis

5 cups chopped kale leaves

2 cups chopped lettuce leaves

1 green apple, peeled, cored and diced

½ teaspoon sea salt

1 tablespoon olive oil

1 tablespoon honey

1 tablespoon balsamic vinegar

½ teaspoon Dijon mustard

Directions:

Whisk together the mustard, vinegar, oil, honey and sea salt. Set aside the vinaigrette.

Spiralize the zucchinis into ribbons by using Blade A. Place the zucchini ribbons in a salad bowl then add the kale, lettuce and apples. Pour in the prepared vinaigrette and toss the ingredients together.

Chill the salad for 30 minutes then serve.

Creamy Veggie Tuna Casserole

Unlike heavy and high-fat versions, this tuna casserole uses light and nutrient-dense zucchini noodles smothered in a creamy coconut milk-based sauce that will satisfy your tummy.

Serves: 4

Ready in: 50 minutes

Ingredients:

3 medium zucchinis, edges trimmed off

2 cans tuna chunks in water

2 cups button mushrooms, halved

1 cup coconut milk

2 tablespoons coconut oil

2 cups grated Parmesan cheese

½ white onion, chopped

2 teaspoons freshly-chopped parsley

½ teaspoon white pepper

1 teaspoon salt

Directions:

Prepare a medium-sized baking dish then preheat the oven to 375°F.

Mount the zucchini in a spiralizer and process it using Blade C. Set the noodles aside.

Heat the coconut oil in a large pan over medium flame. Add in the onions and mushrooms and cook these for 3 minutes. Once the onions are translucent, pour the coconut milk into the pan. Add in the tuna flakes, parsley, salt and pepper. Stir the dish while cooking for 1-2 minutes. Blend in a cup of the cheese then turn off the heat.

Place the zucchini noodles into the sauce then stir until the noodles are well-coated. Transfer the casserole into the baking dish then sprinkle the remaining cheese on top. Cover the baking dish with tin foil then place it in the oven. Bake for 40 minutes.

Mediterranean Zoodle Platter

Tomatoes, capers and sun-dried tomatoes add clean, Mediterranean flavors to crisp zucchini noodles, or "zoodles."

Serves: 4

Ready in: 1 hour

Ingredients:

4 zucchinis, peeled

5 boneless, skinless chicken breast halves, pounded

¼ cup sun-dried tomatoes, chopped

2 strips bacon, chopped

¾ cup artichoke hearts, chopped

½ cup chopped flat parsley

1 tablespoon capers

¼ teaspoon salt

½ teaspoon lemon juice

Directions:

Cook the bacon in a pan over medium-high flame until it becomes golden brown. Remove the bacon from the pan and set aside.

Place the chicken breasts in the pan and fry each side in the bacon fat for 5-7 minutes. Remove the chicken from the pan and lay it on paper towels to absorb the excess oil. Discard the remaining oil from the pan and place it on the stovetop.

While the chicken breasts are being cooked, place the zucchinis through a spiralizer, using Blade B. Set the zoodles aside.

Once the bacon fat has been discarded, place the zoodles on the same pan and cook for 5 minutes. Add the capers, sun-dried tomatoes and artichoke hearts then season with salt. Toss then turn off the heat.

Transfer the zucchini mixture on a plate then sprinkle parsley and chopped bacon on top. Place the chicken breasts on top of the zoodles, drizzle lemon juice all over the dish then serve immediately.

Vegan Lime Pesto with Zucchini

Enjoy the organic yet sprightly flavors of zucchini noodles smothered in a basil and lime pesto sauce. This is a perfect vegan dinner to cap off a hard day's work.

Serves: 3

Ready in: 15 minutes

Ingredients:

2 zucchinis, edges trimmed off

1 cup cherry tomatoes, halved

1 cup button mushrooms, halved

2 cups fresh basil leaves

¼ cup extra virgin olive oil

1 tablespoon unsweetened butter

1 garlic clove

½ teaspoon sea salt

1 teaspoon lime juice

¼ cup pine nuts, toasted

¼ teaspoon red pepper flakes

Directions:

Spiralize your zucchinis by using Blade B of the device. Place the noodles in a microwave safe dish and place it in the microwave. Cook on medium-high for 2 minutes then drain the excess liquid. Set this aside.

Mix together the basil leaves, pine nuts, garlic, butter, lime juice and salt in a blender. Pulse 2 to 3 times then pour in the olive oil. Process the pesto for 30 seconds or until the desired consistency is reached.

Place the zucchini noodles, pesto sauce, tomatoes and mushrooms in a large serving bowl and toss. Serve warm.

Summer Zucchini and Olive Salad

Create this delicious vegetable salad that is best served cold on a hot, summer day. Moreover, the zucchini provides additional electrolytes that will help hydrate the body.

Serves: 4

Ready in: 40 minutes

Ingredients:

2 zucchinis, edges trimmed off

½ cup ricotta cheese

½ cup pitted olives, halved

2 garlic cloves, minced

2 teaspoons lemon juice

½ teaspoon pepper flakes

¼ teaspoon garlic powder

½ tablespoon olive oil

Pinch of salt and pepper

Directions:

Create zucchini ribbons by processing the zucchinis in a spiralizer while using Blade A. Season the ribbons with pepper and set aside.

Heat the olive oil in a pan over medium heat. Add the garlic and pepper flakes and cook for 20 seconds. Mix in the zucchini ribbons and cook for 3-5 minutes. Season the vegetables with salt and garlic powder.

Place the zucchini in a bowl and toss in the ricotta cheese and olives. Cover the bowl with plastic wrap then place it in the fridge. Chill the salad for 30 minutes before serving.

Spiralized Zucchini Rice with Sweet Cider Dressing

Each spoonful of this vegetable rice recipe contains good carbs, protein, fiber and healthy fats that will fill up the stomach without packing on the pounds.

Serves: 4

Ready in: 30 minutes

Ingredients:

2 large zucchinis, edges trimmed off

½ cup dried apricots, roughly chopped

6 strips of bacon

½ cup cottage cheese

¾ cup chopped almonds

2 tablespoons raisins

1 tablespoon maple syrup

1 ½ tablespoon apple cider vinegar

1 teaspoon mustard

½ tablespoon olive oil

Pinch of sea salt and pepper

Directions:

Use Blade C to create thin zucchini noodles. Place the noodles in a chopping board then roughly chop the vegetables into grain-like pieces. Set this aside.

Cook the bacon strips in a pan over medium-high flame for 7 minutes. Once the bacon is crisp, transfer it to a chopping board the mince it. Set the bacon aside.

In a small bowl, whisk together the olive oil, mustard, apple cider vinegar and maple syrup. Set the vinaigrette aside.

Place the zucchini rice, almonds, raisins, apricots and cheese in a large bowl. Pour in the vinaigrette and mix well. Serve the rice in individual bowls then sprinkle the minced bacon on top of each portion before serving.

Vegan Collard Green Wrap

Nothing promotes good health more than a vegetable wrap that's packed with organic nutrients and fresh flavors that will convince you to go meat-free more often.

Serves: 5

Ready in: 30 minutes

Ingredients:

1 large zucchini

1 bell pepper, deseeded and sliced thinly

1 cucumber

½ cup shredded lettuce

¼ cup cilantro leaves

5 large collard green leaves, stem-free

2 tablespoons water

1 ½ tablespoon lemon juice

1 teaspoon grated ginger

½ cup almond butter

1 garlic clove, crushed

2 tablespoons coconut aminos

1 teaspoon honey

Directions:

Spiralize the zucchini and cucumber while using Blade C. Trim the vegetables into 2-inch strands and set aside.

Place the honey, coconut aminos, garlic, ginger, lemon juice, water and almond butter in a blender and pulse until smooth. Pour the nut sauce in a small bowl and set aside.

Get a collard green leaf then spread a spoonful of the nut butter on the leaf. Layer the zucchini noodles, cucumber noodles, lettuce, cilantro and bell pepper on top of the nut sauce then roll the dish into a burrito-like form. Do the same process for the remaining ingredients.

Slice the vegetable wraps diagonally in two then serve it with the remaining peanut sauce for dipping.

Chapter 5 Beet Recipes

Beet Noodles with Tangy Mustard Dressing

Add some flair to clean beet flavors by seasoning it with a taste-bud tingling mustard, maple syrup and vinegar glaze.

Serves: 6

Ready in: 30 minutes

Ingredients:

4 large beets, peeled

15 shallots, peeled and sliced

¾ cup olive oil

4 cups sparkling water

½ cup apple cider vinegar

2 teaspoons Dijon mustard

3 tablespoons maple syrup

Pinch of salt and ground black pepper

Directions:

Preheat the oven to 425°F and prepare a large baking tray.

Drizzle ¼ cup of olive oil into the tray. Using Blade C, process the beets through the spiralizer and place them in the baking tray. Season the noodles with salt, pepper and ½ cup of olive oil. Roast the dish in the oven for 8 minutes.

While the noodles are roasting, heat the remaining olive oil in a medium saucepan over medium heat. Add in the shallots then sauté for 3 minutes. Transfer the cooked shallots to a small plate and set aside.

Pour the sparkling water, apple cider vinegar, maple syrup and mustard into the saucepan and adjust the heat to medium-high. Simmer the mixture for 12-15 minutes until a thick glaze forms. Once the mixture reduces and thickens, stir the glaze continuously for 1 minute to prevent it from sticking to the pan. Turn off the heat then allow the glaze to cool for 2 minutes.

Transfer the roasted beet noodles to a large salad bowl then drizzle the mustard glaze over it. Toss the ingredients together then serve immediately.

Beet Pasta with Creamy Pumpkin Sauce

If you love pasta in Alfredo sauce, try this paleo-friendly alternative that uses pureed pumpkin as a dairy-free substitute for creamy sauces that are high in calories.

Serves: 6

Ready in: 45 minutes

Ingredients:

4 beets, trimmed and peeled

½ tablespoon olive oil

3 sage leaves

¾ cup homemade chicken broth

2 garlic cloves, crushed

¼ cup chopped shallots

½ cup pumpkin puree

¼ teaspoon nutmeg

¼ teaspoon cinnamon powder

Pinch of chili pepper flakes

½ cup cashews, pre-soaked in water for 30 minutes

2 tablespoons freshly-chopped parsley

Pinch of sea salt and pepper

1 tablespoon toasted sesame seeds

Directions:

Create beet noodles by using Blade C to spiralize it. Trim the pasta into 2-inch strands then set aside.

Preheat the oven to 425°F and prepare a parchment-lined baking sheet.

Place the beet pasta on the baking sheet and bake them in the oven for 8 minutes.

While the beets are in the oven, heat the oil in a large skillet over medium-high heat. Add in the sage and fry it for 30 seconds. Remove the sage leaves from the skillet and transfer it to a plate.

In the same skillet, place the garlic, pepper flakes and onion then cook for 2 minutes. Pour in the pumpkin puree then season it with salt, pepper, nutmeg and cinnamon. Let the sauce cook for 2-3 minutes then pour it into the blender.

Drain the cashews then place them in the blender. Pour in the broth, cover the blender then process for 30 seconds. Set this aside.

Take out the beet pasta from the oven and place them in individual bowls. Spoon the pumpkin sauce over each bowl. Sprinkle sesame seeds and parsley on top of each portion before serving.

Chunky Beet and Melon Soup

You can use any type of melon to create a cold soup, but watermelon suits this recipe the best due to its intense sweetness that balances out the organic flavors of the beet noodles.

Serves: 4

Ready in: 30 minutes

Ingredients:

2 medium beets, peeled

4 cups chopped watermelon, deseeded

1 small red onion, chopped

½ cup tomato puree

½ cucumber, peeled and diced

2 tablespoons lime juice

½ jalapeno, chopped

1 tablespoon red-wine vinegar

1 tablespoon apple cider vinegar

½ cup freshly-chopped basil

1 tablespoon olive oil

Pinch of sea salt and pepper

Directions:

Place the watermelon, onion, tomato puree, cucumber, lime juice, jalapeno, vinegars, basil and olive oil in a blender and mix for 1 minute. Season the soup with salt and pepper then mix for another 10 seconds.

Pour the soup in a container and chill in the fridge for 1 hour.

While the soup is being chilled, spiralize your beets by using Blade C of your kitchen device. Set this aside.

To serve, pour the cold soup in individual bowls then place a generous amount of beet noodles on top. Serve immediately.

Beet Caprese Pasta

Level up an Italian Caprese salad by adding some fresh beet noodles that will satiate the stomach and satisfy even the pickiest of taste buds.

Serves: 2

Ready in: 30 minutes

Ingredients:

2 beets, peeled

2 cups torn mozzarella cheese

1 tablespoon olive oil

10 cherry tomatoes, halved

2 garlic cloves, sliced

2 tablespoons freshly-chopped parsley

Pinch of sea salt and ground black pepper

Directions:

Preheat the oven to 400°F and prepare 2 small baking dishes.

Spiralize the beets into long, thin noodles by using the device's Blade C. Set this aside.

Place the tomatoes in a baking dish, season them with salt and pepper then drizzle olive oil over it. Roast the tomatoes for 15 minutes. 10 minutes into roasting, add the sliced garlic to the tray and finish the roasting process.

In another baking dish, add the beet noodles and roast it in the same oven for 5 minutes. After 5 minutes, take out the dish from the oven; place the mozzarella pieces on top of the noodles then roast for another 5 minutes.

Take out the beet noodles with the melted mozzarella and allow it to cool. Get the roasted tomatoes and garlic from the oven and arrange them on top of the noodles. Sprinkle chopped parsley on top of the dish and serve immediately.

Beet Rice Wrap with Pesto Sauce

If you love burritos, try this paleo-friendly wrap that mixes beet rice with chicken, spices and a nutty basil and Parmesan pesto. You will realize that healthy eating can be enjoyable and flavorful, too.

Serves: 4

Ready in: 30 minutes

Ingredients:

1 large beet, peeled

Leaves from 2 lettuce heads

1 ½ cup lean ground turkey meat

2 garlic cloves, minced

1 small red onion, minced

¼ cup water

2 tablespoons butter

1 teaspoon oregano flakes

½ teaspoon red pepper flakes

4 cups fresh basil leaves

½ cup olive oil

½ cup almonds

1 tablespoon minced garlic

Pinch of sea salt and pepper

Directions:

Place the beet in a spiralizer, process with Blade C then place it in a food processor. Process the beet noodles until small grains form. Set these aside.

In a blender, process the basil leaves, garlic, salt, pepper, almonds and olive oil for 1 minute or until a smooth pesto is produced. Set this aside.

Heat the butter in a non-stick pan over medium-high flame. Add the garlic and onion then cook for 2 minutes. Mix in ground turkey, oregano and red pepper flakes then continue cooking for 7 minutes. Pour in the water and allow the liquid to reduce.

Once the liquid has reduced from the pan, fold in the beet rice and mix well. Cook the dish for 5 minutes then pour in the pesto sauce. Cook for 1 minute then turn off the heat.

Place a tablespoon of the beet rice mixture into a lettuce leaf then roll it burrito-style. Do the same process for the rest of the ingredients. Secure with toothpicks if necessary.

Breakfast Beet and Egg Bowl

Start the day with a vitamin-packed breakfast bowl that blends the wonderful flavors and textures of beet rice, eggs, miso paste and kale.

Serves: 2

Ready in: 20 minutes

Ingredients:

2 small beets, peeled

2 eggs, cooked sunny-side up

2 cups chopped kale leaves

1 cup chopped green onions

1 tablespoon water

1 tablespoon miso paste

½ teaspoon grated ginger

1 ½ teaspoons honey

1 tablespoons white vinegar

1 tablespoon olive oil

1 teaspoon toasted sesame seeds

Directions:

Spiralize the beet by using Blade C. Transfer the beet noodles to a chopping board and roughly chop the noodles into small grains. Place the beet rice in a mixing bowl and set this aside.

Whisk together the miso paste, water, vinegar, honey, olive oil and ginger. Set this aside.

Place a large pan over medium-high flame. Add the kale leaves and cook for 3 minutes.

Blend the miso dressing and kale into the beet rice and toss. Place the rice mixture in two bowls. Place a fried egg on top of each bowl then sprinkle sesame seeds and green onions. Serve immediately.

Avocado and Beet Omelet

Don't be scared of ending up with a purple-colored egg dish: its nutritional content and delicious flavor will convince you to not judge a book, or an omelet, by its cover.

Serves: 2

Ready in: 30 minutes

Ingredients:

1 small beet, peeled

4 eggs, beaten

5 tablespoons crumbled cottage cheese

½ avocado, peeled, pitted and sliced

1 tablespoon olive oil

Pinch of sea salt and ground black pepper

Chopped parsley for garnish

Directions:

Using Blade C, spiralize the beet then trim it into 1.5 inch long strands.

Heat the oil in a large pan over medium flame. Add in the beet strands and cook for 5 minutes. Remove the beets from the pan and set aside.

Pour in the eggs into the pan and allow it to set for 1 minute. Season the egg with salt and pepper then place the avocado, cheese and beet noodles in one side of the omelet. Flip over the empty side of the egg and press down the omelet. Let it cook for 2 minutes.

Transfer the omelet onto a serving plate then garnish with chopped parsley. Serve immediately.

Zesty Beets and Bean Pickles

Serve this beet and bean pickled recipe on your next dinner party: the acidity of the dish will liven up everyone's palates and prepare their taste buds for the main course.

Serves: 4

Ready in: 1 hour 15 minutes

Ingredients:

2 beets, peeled

1 tablespoons olive oil

½ cup apple cider vinegar

200 grams wax beans, trimmed and halved

2 tablespoons sugar

1/3 cup freshly-chopped chives

¼ teaspoon sea salt

1/3 cup crumbled cottage cheese

Directions:

Place the beets through a spiralizer while using Blade C. Trim the noodles to 2 to 3-inch strands then set aside.

Place water inside a saucepan, filling up ¾ of the pot. Boil the water over high flame then add the beet noodles and wax beans. Boil the vegetables for 5 minutes then place them in a bowl filled with ice-cold water. Leave it there for 30 seconds then drain the bowl completely.

With the veggies inside the bowl, add the olive oil, vinegar, salt and sugar. Toss the ingredients together then transfer the pickle mixture in an airtight container. Chill the pickled dish in the fridge for 1 hour.

After 1 hour, use a set of tongs to place the beets and beans in a bowl. Pour half of the vinegar juice onto the vegetables. Add the chives and cheese into the bowl then toss. Serve immediately.

Stir-Fried Red Rice with Herbs, Nuts and Cheese

This spiralized beet dish is simply appetizing: it delivers scrumptious flavors from the subtle mix of melted Parmesan, thyme and hazelnuts.

Serves: 2

Ready in: 30 minutes

Ingredients:

2 medium beets, peeled

1 teaspoon fresh thyme leaves

½ cup finely chopped hazelnuts, toasted

¼ cup water

1 garlic clove, crushed

2 tablespoons chopped shallots

1 tablespoon olive oil

¼ cup grated Parmesan cheese

Pinch of salt and ground black pepper

Directions:

Mount the beets in the spiralizer and use Blade C to create long noodles. Place the beet noodles in a food processor and pulse until it becomes grain-like in appearance. Set this aside.

Heat the olive oil in a pan over medium-high flame. Cook the garlic and shallots for 1 minute then add in the beet rice and thyme leaves. Season the dish with salt and pepper, pour in the water then allow the rice to cook for 7 minutes with constant stirring.

After 7 minutes, stir in the Parmesan and hazelnuts. Turn off the heat then plate the rice individually.

Beet, Quinoa and Bean Salad

Enjoy the amazing mix of sweet, tangy and earthy flavors while feasting on this hodgepodge of vegetables, fruit, dairy and protein.

Serves: 4

Ready in: 20 minutes

Ingredients:

2 beets, peeled

1 cup canned corn kernels, drained

½ cup canned pinto beans, drained

1 cup diced avocado meat

¼ cup cilantro leaves

1 cup cooked quinoa

½ cup chopped green bell pepper

8 pieces green olives, pitted and halved

¼ cup cottage cheese

2 tablespoons lemon juice

1 tablespoon vinegar

Pinch of salt and ground black pepper

Directions:

Spiralize the beets into noodles by using Blade C. Place the noodles in a blender and pulse until rice-like pieces are produced.

Place the beet rice in a large mixing bowl. Add in the corn, beans, quinoa, avocado, bell pepper, olives, cilantro and cheese. Pour in lemon juice and vinegar then toss all the ingredients together. Serve immediately or place in the fridge for 30 minutes to chill.

Chapter 6 Sweet Potato Recipes

Low-Calorie Curly Fries

This recipe proves how versatile the spiralizer is by creating thin, spiral fries that are seasoned and baked to perfection.

Serves: 2

Ready in: 30 minutes

Ingredients:

1 large sweet potato, peeled

½ tablespoon garlic powder

¼ cup grated Parmesan cheese

Pinch of salt and ground black pepper

1 tablespoon canola oil

¼ teaspoon freshly chopped parsley

Directions:

Preheat the oven to 425°F and prepare a parchment-lined baking sheet.

Process the sweet potato through the spiralizer while using Blade B. Trim the sweet potato into

3-inch curls then place them in a mixing bowl. Add in the olive oil, cheese, salt, pepper and garlic powder then toss to coat the potato thoroughly.

Lay the potato fries on the baking sheet then place them in the oven. Bake the fries for 10-12 minutes then flip them over. Bake the other side for 5-7 minutes or until the fried become light to golden brown.

Remove the fries from the oven and transfer them to a serving plate. Sprinkle parsley on top before serving.

Gluten Free Spiralized Waffles

Turn your breakfast into a grain-free experience by making this 5-ingredient sweet potato waffle mix that is light, tasty and gut-friendly.

Serves: 2

Ready in: 30 minutes

Ingredients:

2 medium sweet potatoes, peeled

2 eggs, whisked

1 teaspoon cinnamon powder

2 tablespoons honey

1 teaspoon butter

Directions:

Use Blade C to spiralize the sweet potatoes. Set this aside.

Place a non-stick pan over medium flame and melt the butter in it. Add the sweet potato noodles and cook for 10 minutes with constant stirring. Once the noodles are tender, transfer them to a mixing bowl.

Add the eggs and cinnamon powder into the bowl of noodles and mix well.

Coat the waffle iron with cooking spray. Place 1 to 2 tablespoons of the sweet potato mixture into each waffle griddle, making sure to cover the grooves. Cook the waffle for 2-3 minutes then transfer it to a plate.

Serve the waffles warm with a drizzle of honey on top.

Summer Prosciutto and Cottage Cheese Pasta

Bring this delicious sweet potato dish on your next summer camping activity and load up on vitamins and good carbohydrates that are friendly on the waistline.

Serves: 4

Ready in: 30 minutes

Ingredients:

3 small sweet potatoes, peeled

1 cup chopped prosciutto

½ cup cottage cheese

½ cup grated Parmesan cheese

10 dates, pitted and chopped

1 cup almonds, slivered

2 tablespoons water

½ tablespoon coconut oil

Pinch of sea salt

Directions:

Place the sweet potatoes in a spiralizer and use Blade C to create long, thin pasta. Cut the pasta to 1.5-inch long strings and set aside.

Heat the coconut oil in a large pan over medium heat. Add the sweet potato pasta, season it with salt then allow it to cook for 7 minutes. Stir the pasta every few seconds to prevent it from sticking to the pan. Transfer the pasta to a plate.

In the same pan, cook the prosciutto for 3 minutes with constant stirring. Add in the dates, almonds, water and cottage cheese and cook until the cheese has melted. Blend in the sweet potato pasta and stir well.

Transfer the dish to individual plates, sprinkle Parmesan cheese on top then serve immediately.

Vegan Sweet Potato Ribbons with Kale Pesto

Impose a weekly Meatless Monday and include this vegan sweet potato dish in your meal plan: it is full of energy-boosting nutrients and clean, tasty flavors.

Serves: 5

Ready in: 40 minutes

Ingredients:

2 sweet potatoes, peeled

1 bunch kale leaves, stems trimmed off

1 cup walnuts

2 garlic cloves

2 tablespoons vegetable broth

2 tablespoons freshly-chopped parsley

½ teaspoon red pepper flakes

1 tablespoon lemon juice

¼ teaspoon sea salt

2 tablespoons olive oil

Directions:

Spiralize the sweet potatoes while using Blade B. Set the noodles aside.

Place a saucepan with 5 cups of water over high flame and let it boil. Blanch the kale leaves in the boiling water for 2 minutes then remove it from the saucepan. Place the kale leaves in a wire mesh strainer to drain the water from the leaves completely. Set this aside.

Bring the water back to a boil then blanch the sweet potato noodles for 2 minutes. Turn off the heat then drain the water from the noodles completely. Place the sweet potato noodles in a mixing bowl and set aside.

Place the kale, broth and olive oil in a blender and process for 20 seconds. Pour in the lemon juice, salt, pepper flakes, parsley, garlic and walnuts then process for 10 seconds or until the desired consistency is reached.

Pour the green pesto sauce over the sweet potato noodles, mix well then serve immediately.

Sweet Potato Pad Thai

This colorful and healthy sweet potato dish is both dairy and gluten free, making it safe for people with food sensitivities.

Serves: 6

Ready in: 20 minutes

Ingredients:

4 small sweet potatoes, peeled

1 cup roasted almonds, chopped

2 cups fresh bean sprouts

½ cup chopped scallions

2 tablespoons fish sauce

1 tablespoon coconut aminos

¾ cup coconut sugar

½ tablespoon white vinegar

3 tablespoons nut butter

½ teaspoon chili flakes

1 teaspoon tamarind paste

2 tablespoons sesame oil

½ teaspoon garlic powder

Pinch of sea salt

Directions:

Add the fish sauce, coconut aminos, sugar, white vinegar, nut butter, chili flakes, tamarind paste, sesame oil, garlic powder and salt into a saucepan and place it over medium flame. Simmer the mixture for 8 minutes or until the sugar has totally dissolved. Turn off the heat and set aside.

While the sauce is simmering, cut your sweet potato into noodles by using Blade B in your spiralizer. Mix the noodles with the bean sprouts and set aside.

Once the sauce is ready, add the sweet potato noodles and bean sprouts into the saucepan and mix well. Leave it in the sauce for 2-3 minutes to mildly cook the vegetables.

Transfer the Pad Thai into a serving bowl and top it with chopped almonds and scallions before serving.

Spicy Egg and Sweet Potato Bake

Try making this delectable entrée on a weekend brunch with the family: the starch in the sweet potato helps balance the fiery flavors of jalapeno, cumin and paprika.

Serves: 5

Ready in: 30 minutes

Ingredients:

1 large sweet potato, peeled

1 tablespoon olive oil

1 ½ cup diced tomatoes

½ cup chopped onions

1 tablespoon minced garlic

5 eggs

1 tablespoon freshly-chopped cilantro

¼ teaspoon cumin

¼ teaspoon paprika

1 jalapeno pepper, deseeded and chopped

Pinch of sea salt and pepper

Directions:

Preheat the oven to 350°F and lightly grease 5 ramekins with cooking spray.

Spiralize the sweet potato using Blade C and trim the noodles into 2-inch long pieces.

Heat the oil in a pan over medium-high flame. Add the onions, garlic and jalapeno and cook for 3 minutes. Mix in the tomatoes, sweet potato noodles, cumin, paprika, salt and pepper and cook for 7 minutes or until the juices from the chopped tomatoes have thickened. Turn off the heat.

Transfer the sweet potato mixture equally into the ramekins and break an egg on top of each portion. Bake the dish in the oven for 10-12 minutes.

Sprinkle cilantro on top of the dish before serving.

Cheesy Sweet Potato Curls

If you want the little ones to eat their veggies, serve them this organic version of Mac N' Cheese for dinner which uses spiralized sweet potatoes as a gluten free substitute for macaroni.

Serves: 4

Ready in: 30 minutes

Ingredients:

2 medium sweet potatoes, peeled

1 tablespoon almond flour

½ cup almond milk

2 tablespoons butter

½ cup grated cheddar cheese

½ cup grated Parmesan cheese

2 tablespoons freshly-chopped parsley

Directions:

Use Blade B to spiralize the sweet potatoes. Trim the noodles into curls then set aside.

Melt a tablespoon of butter in a deep pan over medium flame. Once the butter has melted, add in the sweet potato curls and cook for 8-10 minutes with constant stirring. Remove the noodles from the pan and set aside.

In the same pan, melt the remaining butter then add in the almond flour. Mix the ingredients to form a roux. Pour in the milk and whisk the mixture until thick.

Add the sweet potato curls into the milk sauce and stir. Finally, mix in the cheddar and Parmesan and stir until the cheese melts. If the sauce is too thick, add a few drops of water or almond milk.

Transfer the dish to a serving plate and sprinkle parsley on top. Serve while hot.

Sweet Potato Wiener Wraps

Serve the kids this quick and fun-looking breakfast of baked lean hotdogs wrapped in long threads of sweet potatoes.

Serves: 8

Ready in: 30 minutes

Ingredients:

2 medium sweet potatoes, peeled

8 lean hotdogs, halved

2 ½ tablespoons butter, melted

1 teaspoon sea salt

Directions:

Preheat the oven to 375°F and prepare a wire rack placed over a baking sheet. Grease the wire rack with half a tablespoon of butter then set aside.

Spiralize the sweet potatoes into long, thin strands by using Blade C. Place the sweet potato strands in a bowl.

Add salt and 2 tablespoons of butter into the sweet potato bowl and toss lightly so as not to damage the strands.

Get half of the hotdog and wrap the sweet potato strands around it. Do not over wrap because you still want to get some crisp after baking the wieners. Do the same for the remaining hotdogs.

Lay the hotdogs on the rack then place it in the oven. Bake for 15-20 minutes then flip the dogs over. Bake the other side for 10 minutes or until the potato wraps become golden brown. Serve immediately.

Spicy Tomato Noodle Soup

Add sweetness and texture to a warm pot of tomato soup by mixing in some sweet potato noodles and diced avocados.

Serves: 2

Ready in: 30 minutes

Ingredients:

1 large sweet potato, peeled

2 cups diced tomatoes

1 cup diced avocadoes

3 cups vegetable broth

½ cup chopped white onions

2 garlic cloves, minced

½ teaspoon cumin

1 tablespoon olive oil

1 tablespoon chili powder

1 tablespoon freshly-chopped cilantro

Directions:

Use Blade C to spiralize the sweet potato. Trim the noodles into 2-inch strands then set aside.

Heat the oil in a saucepan over medium flame. Add the garlic and onion and cook for 2 minutes or until the onions are translucent.

Next, add the tomatoes, chili powder and cumin then season with salt and pepper. Stir the ingredients, cover the pot then allow the tomatoes to simmer for 3 minutes.

After 3 minutes, pour the vegetable broth in the saucepan and adjust the heat to medium-high. Once the soup is boiling, add the sweet potato noodles then reduce the heat back to medium. Simmer the soup for 7 minutes with constant stirring.

Turn off the heat then ladle the soup into individual bowls. Sprinkle the chopped avocado and cilantro on top of the soup before serving.

One-Pot Vegetarian Skillet

Enjoy a flavorful brunch of sweet potato rice, corn, avocados, tomatoes, peppers and beans cooked together in one skillet.

Serves: 3

Ready in: 40 minutes

Ingredients:

1 medium sweet potato, peeled

1 avocado, pitted, peeled and diced

1 cup canned corn kernels, drained

2 garlic cloves, minced

3 eggs, cooked sunny-side up

1 green bell pepper, deseeded and chopped

1 small red onion, minced

3 tomatoes, deseeded and chopped

½ cup black beans

½ teaspoon chili powder

1 tablespoon freshly-chopped cilantro

1 tablespoon olive oil

Directions:

Spiralize the sweet potatoes using Blade C then place the noodles in a food processor. Pulse the noodles until it becomes rice-like in appearance. Set aside.

Heat the olive oil in a large skillet over medium-high flame. Add the onions and garlic then cook for 2 minutes. Mix in the bell peppers then sauté for another minute.

Pour the sweet potato rice into the skillet then mix well. Stir in the tomatoes, cilantro, avocados, black beans and corn kernels. Cover the skillet and cook the dish for 8 minutes.

Once the dish is ready, place the cooked eggs on top of the mixed rice and serve straight from the skillet.

Chapter 7 Healthy Fruit and Vegetable Recipes

Apple and Rhubarb Crisp

Level up your desserts by creating these small but nutrient-dense granola ramekins filled with apple noodles and rhubarb.

Serves: 4

Ready in: 40 minutes

Ingredients:

3 gala apples

4 rhubarb stalks, sliced lengthwise then diced

1 cup granola

4 teaspoons maple syrup

Directions:

Preheat the oven to 375°F and prepare 4 ramekins.

Place your apples in a spiralizer and use Blade C to create strands. Discard the core and place the apple noodles in a bowl. Mix in the diced rhubarb.

Spoon the apple rhubarb mixture into each of the ramekins then drizzle a teaspoon of maple syrup into each ramekin. Place the ramekins in the oven and bake for 20 minutes.

After 20 minutes, take out the ramekins and spoon granola on top of each fruit cup. Place the ramekins back into the oven then bake for 5 minutes. Serve warm.

Pescetarian Cabbage Bowl

Even green leafy vegetables can be spiralized, as shown in this nutritious tuna and cabbage recipe that's perfect for a pescetarian lunch or dinner.

Serves: 2

Ready In: 15 minutes

Ingredients:

1 small head of cabbage

1 tablespoon minced garlic

¼ cup chicken broth

1 ½ cups canned tuna in water

1 pinch chili pepper

1 red onion, chopped

1 tablespoon olive oil

1 tablespoons slivered almonds

Pinch of sea salt and ground black pepper

Directions:

Heat the olive oil in a large pan over medium-high flame. Add in the garlic, onion and chili pepper then cook for 2 minutes.

Spiralize the cabbage by using Blade A. Place the shredded cabbage into the pan and cook while stirring for 3 minutes. Pour the chicken broth and let it simmer for 2 minutes or until the liquid has fully evaporated.

Mix in the tuna and toss the ingredients in the pan for 1 minute. Transfer the dish into individual bowls then top with almonds before serving.

Parmesan Broccoli Noodles with Tomatoes

Pick a large-stemmed broccoli for spiralizing: this will not only make the noodle-making process easier, but it will add more vitamins and clean flavors to your plate.

Serves: 2

Ready in: 30 minutes

Ingredients:

1 broccoli head with 2 or 3-inch diameter stem

1 cup cherry tomato halves

3 garlic cloves, minced

½ teaspoon red pepper flakes

2 tablespoons olive oil

1 tablespoon chopped walnuts

1 tablespoon lemon juice

2 tablespoons grated Parmesan cheese

Pinch of sea salt and ground black pepper

Directions:

Separate the broccoli head from the stem by slicing it. Mount the stem in a spiralizer and slice it into thin noodles while using Blade C. Set the noodles aside. Break the broccoli into small florets.

Heat the olive oil in a large skillet over medium-high flame. Add the pepper flakes, salt, pepper, broccoli florets and noodles and stir. Allow the dish to cook while covered for 5 minutes.

After 5 minutes, add in the tomatoes, lemon juice and garlic then stir. Cook the dish for another 5 minutes then transfer it to a plate. Sprinkle walnuts and Parmesan cheese on top before serving.

Sausage, Spinach and Squash Casserole

Ditch unhealthy, gluten-rich noodles for spiralized butternut squash when making a casserole: this makes for a lighter and digestion-friendly dinner.

Serves: 5

Ready in: 1 hour 30 minutes

Ingredients:

1 butternut squash, bulbous bottom sliced off

5 cups spinach leaves

5 sausage links, cases removed

5 fresh sage leaves

3 garlic cloves, minced

1 small onion, chopped

1 egg, whisked

¼ teaspoon red pepper flakes

½ tablespoon olive oil

Pinch of salt and pepper

1 ½ cups ricotta cheese

1 cup shredded cheddar cheese

1/3 cup grated parmesan cheese

Directions:

Preheat the oven to 400°F and prepare a 4-quart baking dish.

In a small bowl, mix together the parmesan, ricotta and egg. Set this aside.

Peel the butternut squash then slice it into 2. Place each half in the spiralizer and make large slices using Blade A. Set this aside.

Heat the oil and sage leaves in a pan over medium flame, making sure that the leaves do not get burnt. Transfer the sage leaves to a chopping board, mince it then set aside.

On the same pan, cook the sausage meat for 7 minutes or until it turns golden brown. Blend in the garlic, shallots, pepper flakes, salt, pepper and spinach. Cover the pan then let the ingredients cook for 2 minutes.

To assemble the casserole, place a layer of squash slices at the bottom of the baking dish followed by a layer of the spinach mixture. Add a layer of the egg and cheese mixture on top. Make another set of squash, spinach and cheese mixture then place a final layer of squash on top. Sprinkle the cheddar cheese on top of the squash layer then cover the top of the baking dish with tin foil. Place the dish in the oven then bake for 45 minutes.

Remove the tin foil then sprinkle chopped sage on the casserole. Let the dish cool down for 5 minutes before serving.

Gluten-Free Parsnip Puttanesca

Add nutrients and flavor to a classic Italian dish by replacing starchy noodles with spiralized parsnips that perfectly complement the bold flavors of tomatoes and anchovies.

Serves: 4

Ready in: 45 minutes

Ingredients:

4 parsnips, peeled

1 cup diced tomatoes

1 teaspoon tomato paste

3 anchovy fillets, chopped

1 tablespoon capers

3 garlic cloves, minced

1 onion, chopped

1 teaspoon red pepper flakes

½ cup freshly-chopped parsley

½ cup water

Pinch of sea salt and ground black pepper

1 tablespoon coconut oil

Directions:

Spiralize the parsnips into long, thin noodles by utilizing Blade C. Place the vegetable pasta and coconut oil in a large pan then let it cook for 20 minutes over medium-high flame, stirring constantly. Transfer the pasta in a serving platter and let it cool.

On the same pan, sauté the garlic, onions and pepper flakes for 2-3 minutes. Mix in the capers, anchovies, tomatoes, tomato paste and water then let it simmer for 2 minutes. Mix in the chopped parsley then season the sauce with salt and pepper. Turn off the heat.

Pour the puttanesca sauce over the parsnip noodles. Lightly toss the dish then serve immediately.

Rutabaga Spaghetti with Truffle Marinara Sauce

The kids will love this veggie-friendly spin on a classic favorite: the mushrooms, truffle oil and herbs mixed into ready-made marinara sauce will tickle everyone's taste buds.

Serves: 3

Ready in: 30 minutes

Ingredients:

2 rutabagas, peeled and trimmed

½ cup chopped white mushrooms

1 cup ground beef

2 garlic cloves, crushed

1 small onion, minced

1 ½ cup marinara sauce

1 teaspoon truffle oil

1 tablespoon freshly chopped parsley

Pinch of salt and pepper

Directions:

In a large pan, mix together the beef, garlic, onions and mushrooms. Cook the ingredients over medium-high flame for 10 minutes then pour in the marinara sauce. Season the sauce with salt the pepper then allow it to simmer for 15-20 minutes.

Place the rutabagas on a spiralizer then use Blade B to make spaghetti-like pasta. Transfer the pasta into a pot, fill it with water and boil it over high flame for 8 minutes. Drain the pasta and place it on a serving platter. Drizzle the truffle oil over the rutabaga and toss gently.

Once the sauce is done, pour it over the rutabaga pasta. Sprinkle parsley on top then serve.

Warm Turnip Noodle Soup

Add more vitamins to a warm bowl of chicken soup by mixing in some freshly spiralized turnip noodles, carrots and aromatics.

Serves: 4

Ready in: 45 minutes

Ingredients:

1 turnip, edges trimmed and peeled

2 boiled chicken breast halves, deboned and diced

2 carrots, peeled and diced

1 onion, chopped

2 celery stalks, chopped

3 garlic cloves, minced

4 cups homemade chicken broth

1 tablespoon chopped thyme leaves

2 tablespoons unsalted butter

Pinch of sea salt and ground black pepper

Directions:

Grease the inside of a large pot with butter and arrange the chicken, celery, carrots and onions. Cover the pot and cook the ingredients over medium flame for 8-10 minutes.

Add thyme, pepper and salt to the chicken mixture then pour in the broth. Simmer the soup for 30 minutes.

While the soup is cooking, spiralize your turnip, using Blade B. Slice the turnip noodles into 2-inch lengths.

After 30 minutes, add the turnip noodles into the chicken soup and simmer for 5 minutes. Serve while hot.

Asian Radish and Mushroom Stir-Fry

This gluten-free dish mixes Chinese white radish and mushrooms with coconut aminos for a low-calorie and tummy-friendly entrée.

Serves: 5

Ready in: 30 minutes

Ingredients:

1 medium Chinese white radish, trimmed and peeled

10 Shiitake mushrooms, pre-soaked in water for 30 minutes

10-12 pieces snap peas, trimmed

3 green onions, chopped

2 tablespoons coconut aminos

2 tablespoons olive oil

1 teaspoon grated ginger

1 teaspoon sea salt

1 teaspoon white pepper

1 teaspoon brown sugar

Directions:

Squeeze out excess water from the soaked mushrooms. Cut off the stems and discard. Roughly chop the mushroom heads then set aside.

Place the radish in a spiralizer and process it using Blade C. Set the noodles aside.

Heat the olive oil in a pan over medium-high flame. Add in the mushrooms, snap peas, green onions and ginger and stir. Season the vegetables with salt, pepper, brown sugar and a tablespoon of coconut aminos. Cook the veggies for 5 minutes then transfer them to a plate.

Place the radish noodles in the same pan and season it with the remaining coconut aminos. Stir-fry the noodles for 10 minutes then add in the vegetables. Toss gently then transfer the dish to a serving platter.

Crisp Apple and Lettuce Salad

This tangy fruit and vegetable salad is a perfect brunch for those who want subtle hints of organic sweetness into their leafy greens.

Serves: 4

Ready in: 15 minutes

Ingredients:

3 red apples, peeled and cored

5 cups chopped romaine lettuce leaves

½ cup slivered almonds

1/2 cup raisins

2 tablespoons balsamic vinegar

2 tablespoons olive oil

2 teaspoons honey

1 tablespoon Dijon mustard

Pinch of salt and pepper

Directions:

Place the apples in a spiralizer and process it into short noodles by using Blade C. Set this aside.

In a small bowl, whisk together the balsamic vinegar, olive oil, honey, mustard, salt and pepper. Pour the prepared dressing in a salad bowl.

Add the apples and lettuce in the salad bowl and toss them together with the dressing. Sprinkle almonds and raisins then toss lightly. Serve immediately.

Chapter 8 Soup Recipes

Chicken and Zucchini Noodle Soup

Ingredients:

½ cup of spaghetti cut thick zucchini

2 pieces chicken breasts, cubed (skin and bone removed)

5 cups of chicken broth

1 cup low-fat coconut milk

2 pieces jalapeno, finely chopped

2 cloves of garlic, finely chopped

1 ½ inch piece ginger, grated

1 tablespoon lime zest

¼ cup freshly squeezed lime juice

4 tablespoons fish sauce

2 cups shitake mushrooms, sliced

2 cups spinach leaves

2 tablespoons cilantro, chopped

Procedure:

- In medium-sized sauce pan, pour in chicken broth. Add garlic, ginger, and jalapeno. Add lime juice and zest, and 3 tablespoons of fish sauce. Simmer.
- Add in the zucchini noodles. Cook for one minute or until noodles are tender. Remove noodles and place in a bowl. Set aside, covered.
- Add in shitake mushrooms and simmer for another 4 minutes before adding the chicken breasts and coconut milk. Simmer until chicken is cooked.
- Toss in the spinach leaves and stir until leaves become limp.
- Add cilantro and the remaining 1 tablespoon of fish sauce.
- Equally divide zucchini noodles into 4 medium-sized bowls.
- Pour in the soup over the noodles just before serving.
- Serves 4.

Mexican Style Chicken Noodle Soup

Ingredients:

2 cups of zucchini noodles, spaghetti circles

6 cups of chicken stock

2 14-ounce cans of roasted tomatoes

4 pieces chicken breast fillets, (skin and bone removed)

5 cloves of garlic, minced

1 medium-sized yellow onion, chopped

1 large bunch of cilantro, chopped (approx makes 1 cup)

1 jalapeno pepper, minced and seeded

2 medium-sized carrots, chopped into thin circles

Juice of 2 pieces of lime

1 teaspoon cumin

1 teaspoon turmeric

1 teaspoon black pepper

Procedure:

- In a large pot, sauté onions, garlic, and carrots in oil.
- Add canned tomatoes (do not drain). Pour in the chicken stock and chicken breasts. Bring to a boil until chicken breasts is cooked. Remove chicken breasts from the broth and set aside. Allow to cool.
- Simmer broth, covered.
- When the chicken breasts are cool enough to handle, shred into smaller pieces and put back into the pot. Add the zucchini noodles, lime juice, and spices. Simmer for 30 seconds.
- Serves 6.

Vietnamese Pho Soup Simplified

Ingredients:

2 cups of yellow squash noodles

8 cups of low-sodium beef broth

4 cups of water

¾ lb thinly-sliced flank steak

1 medium-sized yellow onion, sliced

5 cloves of garlic, minced

1 piece 2-inch ginger, grated

2 whole cloves of garlic

1 cinnamon stick

2 tablespoons fish sauce

Green onions, finely chopped

Jalapeno peppers, thinly sliced

Cilantro, chopped

Lime wedges

Procedure:

- In a large pot, bring to a boil over high heat, the beef broth, water, and spices. When boiling, cover pan and reduce heat. Simmer for 30 minutes while stirring occasionally.
- Add squash noodles and beef flanks to the pot. Bring to a boil until beef is cooked. If you sliced the beef as thinly as possible, cooking time will only be 1 to 2 minutes.
- Remove cinnamon stick just before serving.
- Garnish with green onions, jalapeno peppers, cilantro, and lime wedges per serving bowls.
- Makes 4.

Cauliflower Rice Soup

Ingredients:

2/3 cup of cauliflower florets, "rice" cut

3 cups of chicken broth

¼ cup of baby shrimps

1 piece chicken breast fillet, cut into cubes

2 tablespoons of water chestnuts, chopped

¼ cup of bamboo shoots

½ cup of shitake mushrooms, sliced

½ cup of bean sprouts

1 large egg

2 cups of canola oil

1 tablespoon of dry sherry

4 tablespoons of cornstarch

Procedure:

- In a mixing bowl, slightly beat the egg and mix with cornstarch. Coat the shrimps and chicken pieces thoroughly.
- In a frying pan, heat 1 ½ cups of oil.

- Stir-fry the coated shrimps and chicken pieces until cooked. Remove from the pain, drain oil, and set aside.
- In a large sauce pan, mix in chicken broth, bamboo shoots, and mushrooms, and bring to a boil.
- Pour in the sherry and reduce heat. Simmer.
- Re-heat oil in the frying pan and quickly cook the cauliflower "rice" until golden brown. Remove from pan and drain excess oil.
- Add the cauliflower "rice" and the bean sprouts to the soup.
- Makes 8.

High-Fiber Noodle Soup

Ingredients:

2 cups of zucchini noodles (or yellow squash), spaghetti cut

2 cans of vegetable broth (14 ounces each)

1 jar of salsa (16 ounces)

1 can black beans, drained and rinsed (15-ounces)

2 cups of corn kernels (use frozen and not canned)

Juice extract of 1 piece lime

2 teaspoons of chili powder

½ teaspoon of cumin

Procedure:

- In a medium-sized sauce pan, pour in vegetable broth and bring to a boil.
- Add all the other ingredients.
- Cook for another 1 to 2 minutes, or until the vegetables are tender.
- Serves 6.

Zucchini Noodle Soup with Bok Choy and Shrimps

Ingredients:

3 cups of zucchini pasta, spaghetti cut

1 ½ cups of seafood stock or clam juice

6 cups of chicken stock

2 pounds raw shrimps (deveined and shelled)

1 large Bok Choy, sliced thinly

3 pieces green onions, sliced thinly

1 tablespoons red pepper flakes, crushed

2 tablespoons grated ginger

3 large cloves of garlic, minced

1/3 pound shitake mushrooms, sliced

3 tablespoons of canola oil

Procedure:

- In a large pot, heat oil and add Bok Choy, mushrooms, ginger, garlic, and pepper flakes. Set to medium heat for 1 minute, before adding clam juice and chicken stock. Bring to a boil, covered.

- When stock is boiling, drop the shrimps. Add the green onions.
- Add in the noodles just before removing from heat.
- Let it stand for 5 minutes before serving.
- Serves 6 top 8.

Rich Pumpkin Soup

Ingredients:

4 cups of pumpkin noodles, flat cut

5 cups of vegetable broth

1 large can (29-ounces) of pumpkin puree

1 large yellow onion, diced

2 tablespoons of olive oil

2 tablespoons of brown sugar

2 teaspoons of dried sage (or 2 tablespoons of fresh sage, chopped)

1 teaspoon cinnamon

¼ teaspoon ginger

¼ teaspoon cayenne pepper

1/8 teaspoon nutmeg

Procedure:

- In a large sauce pan heat oil and cook onions, and then add in the spices.
- Add in the pumpkin puree.

- Pour in the vegetable broth and bring a boil. Once boiling, reduce heat and simmer.
- Add in the brown sugar.
- Toss in the pumpkin noodles. Simmer for 2 to 3 minutes more.
- Serves 6 individuals.

Note: If you are on a strict Paleo diet, omit the brown sugar.

Minestrone with a Twist

Ingredients:

1 cup of zucchini pasta (you can also use yellow squash), spaghetti circles cut

4 cups of chicken broth

1 can crushed tomatoes (28 ounces)

1 can cannellini beans, drained and rinsed (15 ounces)

1 cup escarole (you can also use kale), shredded

2 large carrots, thin circles

2 ribs celery, diced

1 yellow onion, chopped

3 cloves of garlic, minced

2 teaspoons of Italian seasoning

Parmesan cheese, grated (optional)

Procedure:

- In a slow cooker, pour in the chicken broth and canned tomatoes (do not drain). Add in carrots, garlic, onions, and celery. Pour in Italian seasoning.

- Cover and cook for 4 to 6 hours, at low setting.
- After about 6 hours, add in the escarole and beans. Cover. Increase heat and cook for another 10 minutes or until the newly added veggies are cooked.
- Add in the zucchini noodles. Cook for 2 minutes more.
- Serve immediately.
- You can garnish with parmesan cheese if you want.

Asian Inspired Chicken Salad

Chicken and noodles make a hearty soup but this recipe gives you a delicious and unique Asian-inspired salad.

Ingredients:

 3 cups of zucchini noodles (you can also use yellow squash), flat cut

 2 cups of chicken breast fillet, bite-sized cuts, cooked

 ½ cup of creamy peanut butter

 3 tablespoons of water

 4 tablespoons of gluten-free soy sauce

 3 tablespoons of rice vinegar

 2 tablespoons of chili-garlic sauce

 2 tablespoons of fresh ginger, grated

 1 tablespoon of brown sugar

 1 small bunch of cilantro leaves, chopped

 1 bunch of green onions, thinly sliced

2 medium-sized carrots, grated

1 piece bell pepper, cut in matchsticks

Procedure:

- If you want your noodles to be softer, you can blanch them first, otherwise, just leave your veggie noodles raw.
- In a large salad bowl, put in the noodles, cooked chicken bites, carrots, green onions, bell pepper, and cilantro.
- In a food processor (you can also use a blender if you don't have a food processor), mix peanut butter, brown sugar, chili-garlic sauce, soy sauce, and water. Blend until you get a smooth consistency. Add more water if it becomes too thick.
- Pour the dressing to your chicken and noodle salad and toss. Chill for about one hour before serving.
- Makes 4.

Mediterranean Veggie Salad

Ingredients:

4 cups of zucchini noodles, spaghetti cut

2 cups of chicken breast fillet, bite-sized pieces, cooked

3 pieces medium-sized hard-boiled egg whites, dice

2 cloves of garlic, diced

1 small red onion, dice

3 tablespoons of olive oil

Juice extract of half a lemon

1 teaspoon basil

½ teaspoon dried rosemary

Black olives, sliced, for garnish

If you want to use Greek yogurt or mayonnaise, use only 1 tablespoon of olive oil and add 2 tablespoons of mayonnaise or Greek yogurt.

Procedure:

- For softer noodles, blanch your noodles, or if you prefer raw, then leave it as is.
- In a salad bowl, mix together your noodles, chicken bites, egg whites, and red onions.
- In a small mixing bowl, whisk all the other ingredients. Pour it over your chicken noodle salad and toss.
- You may garnish your salad with fresh olives.
- If you are not on a Paleo Diet, you can add in some crumbled feta cheese.
- This recipe serves 4.

Spicy Orange and Avocado Slaw

Ingredients:

1 medium-sized carrot noodles, spaghetti cut

½ medium cabbage noodles, spaghetti cut

3 pieces scallions, thinly sliced

1 medium-sized avocado, peeled and pitted

3 tablespoons of apple cider vinegar

Zest of ½ orange

Juice of 1 piece orange

2 cloves of garlic, minced

2 tablespoons of olive oil

1 teaspoon of homemade Sriracha (recipe at the end of the book)

½ teaspoon sea salt

¼ teaspoons freshly ground black pepper

Procedure:

- In a large salad bowl, put in carrots, cabbage, and scallions. Blanch the carrots and cabbage noodles first if you want them softer.
- With the use of a food processor or blender, make your dressing by combining avocado, apple cider vinegar, sriracha, olive oil, garlic, sea salt, ground pepper, and orange juice and zest. Blend until smooth.
- Pour over your slaw.
- This recipe is good for 4.

Fruity Cucumber Salad

Ingredients:

2 medium-sized cucumber noodles, peeled, spaghetti cut

1 pint of fresh strawberries, hulled and sliced

2 cups of baby spinach

Juice of 1 piece orange

Zest of ½ orange

¼ cup of olive oil

½ teaspoon of sea salt

¼ teaspoon ground black pepper

½ teaspoon fresh thyme, chopped

Procedure:

- After the cutting the cucumber noodles, drain water and dry using a paper towel before putting them in a large salad bowl. Then add in the fresh strawberries and spinach.

- In a small mixing bowl, put the orange juice and zest, olive oil, apple cider vinegar, thyme, salt, and pepper.
- Pour the vinaigrette dressing to your salad and toss. You can also serve the vinaigrette on the side.
- Serves 4.

Mexican-Flavored Slaw

Ingredients:

½ small head of green cabbage, shredded

½ small head of Napa cabbage, shredded

1 bunch of red radishes, thinly sliced

2 pieces of fresh Poblano chilies (or you can use Hatch or jalapeno), diced

Juice extract of 3 pieces lime

1 tablespoons of canola oil

1 bunch of fresh cilantro leaves, minced

¼ teaspoon of cayenne pepper

Procedure:

- In a salad bowl, combine cabbages and radishes. You can blanch them if you want them softer. Add the diced peppers and set aside.
- In a small mixing bowl, put the lime juice, cayenne pepper, and cilantro. Let

the mixture sit for at least 5 minutes. Whisk in the canola oil.

- Pour the vinaigrette your salad and toss well.
- You can serve it immediately or let it chill for at least an hour.
- This serves 4 to 6.

Carrots and Beets Slaw

Ingredients:

3 large beets noodles, spaghetti cut

4 large carrots noodles, spaghetti cut

2 tablespoons of Dijon mustard

3 tablespoons of red wine vinegar

3 tablespoons of olive oil

1 teaspoon of ground black pepper

Procedure:

- In a serving or salad bowl, arrange the beet and carrot noodles.
- In a small mixing bowl, mix olive oil, red wine vinegar, Dijon mustard, and ground pepper. Whisk thoroughly.
- Pour the vinaigrette over your beet and carrot noodles. Toss lightly.
- Serves 4.

Zucchini and Salmon Salad

Ingredients:

8 cups of zucchini noodles, spaghetti circles cut

1 can of salmon (15 ounces), drained and flaked

1 bunch of fresh dill, minced

2 medium-sized bell peppers, minced, seeds removed

1 cup of olive oil

1/3 cup of Dijon mustard

½ cup red wine vinegar

2 cloves of garlic, minced

Procedure:

- You can blanch the zucchini noodles first if you want it softer, otherwise, you can leave it raw.
- In a large mixing bowl, whisk together olive oil, Dijon mustard, vinegar, and garlic.

- Add in zucchini noodles, bell peppers, and flaked salmon. Toss.

Broccoli Slaw with Almonds

Ingredients:

2 cups of broccoli stems, spaghetti cut

2 cups of broccoli florets, trimmed into smaller florets

1 large carrot noodles, spaghetti cut

½ cup of slivered almonds

1 cup of garlic aioli (get recipe below)

Zest of ½ lemon

Juice extract from 1 lemon

1 teaspoon fresh rosemary, chopped

1 tablespoon fresh thyme, chopped

1 tablespoon fresh chives, chopped

½ teaspoon sea salt

¼ teaspoon ground black pepper

Procedure:

- Put the broccoli florets and carrot and broccoli noodles in a large salad bowl. Add in slivered almonds.
- Whisk together garlic aioli, lemon juice and zest, thyme, rosemary, chives, sea salt, and pepper in a small mixing bowl.
- Pour in the dressing and toss to combine.

Flavorful Daikon Radish Fries

Ingredients:

1 daikon radish noodles, cut into strands

2 tablespoons of melted coconut oil

1 teaspoon Sriracha

1 teaspoon of wheat-free tamari (you can use coconut aminos)

¼ teaspoon of stevia

½ teaspoon of fresh ginger, grated

1 clove of garlic, minced

½ teaspoon of sea salt

Procedure:

- Preheat your oven to 475°F.
- Line your baking dish with parchment paper.

- Put the radish strands in a large mixing bowl.
- Whisk together sriracha, coconut oil, tamari, ginger, garlic, sea salt, and stevia in a small mixing bowl.
- Drizzle your dressing evenly over your daikon radishes and toss.
- Arrange the daikon radishes on your baking dish. Bake for about 20 to 30 minutes or until golden brown. Don't forget to stir once or twice while baking.
- This recipe serves 2.

Veggie Side in Balsamic Vinegar

Ingredients:

4 medium-sized carrots, spaghetti circles cut

2 medium-sized turnips, julienned

2 yellow squash noodles, spaghetti circles cut

2 medium-sized red bell peppers, seeds removed, julienned

1 piece large yellow onion, thinly sliced

1 bunch of fresh rosemary, chopped

4 fresh sage leaves, chopped (or substitute with 1 teaspoon dried sage)

1 tablespoon Italian seasoning

3 large cloves of garlic, minced

3 tablespoons of balsamic vinegar

1 teaspoon ground black pepper

3 tablespoons of canola oil

Procedure:

- In a large skillet, sauté the vegetables in canola oil until they are crispy.
- In a small mixing bowl, combine the balsamic vinegar and the remaining ingredients. Mix thoroughly before pouring over the sautéed vegetables in the skillet.
- Cook for 5 minutes more stirring occasionally to blend the flavors well.
- This serves 8 to 10.

Simple Squash Sauté

This is a simple sautéed side dish that even budding home cooks can prepare on their own.

Ingredients:

2 pounds summer squash noodles, spaghetti or matchstick cut

(you can also mix with zucchini noodles for more color, just make it 1 pound each)

1 pound Roma tomatoes, ripe, thinly sliced

1 yellow onion, medium-sized, thinly sliced

3 tablespoons of olive oil

2 large cloves of garlic, minced

½ teaspoon of dried red pepper flakes, crushed

1 tablespoon of Italian seasoning

Grated parmesan cheese

Procedure:

- Grease a large pan. Heat and then sauté garlic and onion.
- When the onion slices are translucent, add in the Roma tomatoes. Sauté until the tomatoes release their juices.
- Add in the squash noodles (or squash and zucchini noodles) and cook for another 2 minutes.
- Add in the red pepper flakes and Italian seasoning.
- Top with parmesan cheese if you want.
- Serves 8.

Potato Casserole

Ingredients:

4 cups of potatoes, julienned or spaghetti circles cut

2 cups of sliced mushrooms

2 cups of chicken broth

1 medium-sized yellow onion, chopped

1 large clove of garlic, minced

1 pack of frozen spinach, chopped (thawed, drained, and squeezed of excess water)

2 ½ cups of low fat milk

1 tablespoon of olive oil

1/3 cup cheese, shredded

½ teaspoon ground black pepper

2 medium-sized eggs, lightly beaten

2 teaspoons off cornstarch

Parmesan cheese, grated

Procedure:

- Preheat your oven to 350°F.
- Coat an 11x7 baking dish with butter or oil. You can also use cooking spray.
- In a large pan, sauté garlic, onions, and mushrooms in olive oil.
- Gently pour in the chicken broth and ground black pepper. Simmer in medium to high heat until broth is reduced.
- Add in the spinach.
- Arrange potato slices in the baking dish. Cover with the spinach and mushroom mixture.
- Cover with half of the cheese.
- Add another layer potato slices, and then the spinach and mushroom mixture.
- In small mixing bowl, whisk together the milk, eggs, and cornstarch. Pour over the potato layers; make sure that the mixture is evenly distributed.
- Bake in the oven 1 ½ hours.
- Top the casserole with the remaining cheese and put back in the oven to bake for another 20 minutes or until cheese becomes bubbly and golden brown.
- You may garnish with parmesan cheese.
- This serves 6.

Asian Noodles

Ingredients:

4 cups of zucchini noodles (yellow squash can also be used), spaghetti cut

1 bunch of green onions, thinly sliced

4 large cloves of garlic, minced

3 tablespoons of honey

¼ cup of gluten-free soy sauce

1/3 cup of rice vinegar

1/3 cup of olive oil

2 tablespoons of sesame oil

1 tablespoon of red pepper, crushed

1 tablespoon of sesame seeds, lightly toasted

Procedure:

- Blanch the zucchini noodles if you want them softer or leave them at that, place them in a large bowl.

- In a small sauce pan, mix canola oil and sesame oil. Add vinegar, honey, and soy sauce. Bring to a boil. Add the red pepper.
- Just before serving, pour the hot soup into the bowl with the noodles.
- Top with green onions and sesame seeds.
- Makes 8 servings.

Vegetable Pasta with Bacon Bits

Ingredients:

4 cups of yellow squash noodles (or zucchini noodles), spaghetti cut

¾ pound bacon, crispy bits

1 large yellow onion, thinly sliced

2 large bunches of Swiss chard (stem and ribs removed), chopped

3 tablespoons of olive oil

¾ cup parmesan cheese, grated

Procedure:

- Blanch the yellow squash noodles. Save one cup of the liquid. Place the noodles in a serving bowl.
- In a large non-stick pan, brown the bacon until crispy. Remove from pan and drain excess oil. Leave about 3 tablespoons of bacon fat in the pan.
- Add in onions and cook until soft and translucent. Then add the Swiss chard and the liquid from blanching. When

char has wilted, remove from heat and pour over the yellow squash noodles.

- Sprinkle the bacon bits over your vegetable pasta.
- Top with parmesan cheese but if you into Paleo diet, ditch the cheese.
- This recipe makes 4 servings.

3-Flavor Raw Cucumber Noodles

Ingredients:

2 medium-sized cucumber noodles, spaghetti cut

2 pieces scallions, thinly sliced (use the white and green parts)

2 tablespoons of sesame seeds, toasted

¼ cup of olive oil

1 teaspoon of sesame oil

½ teaspoon of chili oil

2 tablespoons of rice vinegar

½ teaspoon orange zest

1 tablespoon of orange juice

1 clove of garlic, minced

½ teaspoon of fresh ginger, grated

¼ teaspoon of sea salt

¼ teaspoon of stevia

Procedure:

- Remove excess water from the cucumber noodles by patting them dry with paper towels.
- In a large mixing bowl, place the cucumber noodles and scallions. Add in sesame seeds and mix.
- In a smaller mixing bowl, whisk olive oil, sesame oil, chili oil, orange zest and juice, vinegar, garlic, ginger, stevia, and sea salt.
- Pour vinaigrette into the cucumber noodles and toss.
- Serves 2. You can adjust the measurements if you need more.

Sweet Potato Chips Ribbons with Raita Dip

Ingredients:

Chips

1 large sweet potato (peeled), ribbon noodles cut

2 tablespoons of melted coconut oil

1 teaspoon curry powder

½ teaspoon sea salt

Raita Dip

2 cups plain yogurt

Juice extract of 1 lemon

1 piece cucumber noodles, spaghetti cut

½ teaspoon sea salt

Procedure:

For the chips:

- Preheat your oven to 400°F.

- Line a baking sheet with parchment paper or brush with butter or oil.
- In a mixing bowl, place the sweet potato chips, add in coconut oil, curry power, and sea salt. Mix well.
- Arrange the sweet potato noodles on the baking sheet. Bake in the oven for 15 minutes or until chips are crispy. Remove from the oven.
- Let it cool while on the baking sheet.
- Once completely cooled, transfer to a serving bowl.

For the raita dip:

- Whisk plain yogurt and lemon juice in a mixing bowl.
- With the use of a food processor, pulse the cucumber noodles until you get consistency similar to rice.
- Mix the processed cucumber noodles with the yogurt and lemon juice mixture. Add in sea salt.

You can replace the curry powder with garlic powder or Italian seasoning if you want. You can easily experiment with the spices so explore, there are a variety of choices out there.

Zucchini Pasta with Shrimp Fra Diavolo

Ingredients:

For the noodles

6 medium-sized zucchini noodles, spaghetti cut

3 tablespoons of canola oil

For the shrimp

1 pound of fresh shrimps, deveined and peeled

1 teaspoon of red pepper flakes, crushed

½ teaspoon sea sat

4 tablespoons of olive

1 medium-sized onion, chopped

3 cloves of garlic, minced

1 cup white wine

1 can diced tomatoes, un-drained (14 ounces)

½ teaspoon of oregano powder

¼ teaspoon of ground black pepper

3 tablespoons of parsley, chopped (fresh)

Procedure:

For the noodles:

- In a skillet, heat canola oil and cook the zucchini noodles, with constant stirring, for about 5 minutes.
- Set aside.

For the shrimps:

- In a mixing bowl, place the shrimps and add the red pepper flakes and sea salt. Mix and then let it sit for 10 minutes.
- While waiting, heat half of the olive in large pan over medium to high heat.
- Add the shrimps, with constant stirring, until they turn pink. This may take about 4 minutes. Remove from pan and transfer to a planter. Cover with aluminum foil.
- Pour in the remaining half of the olive oil into the pan. Add onions and cook for about 5 minutes, then add in the garlic.

- Pour in white wine and cook. This may take about 3 minutes. Scrape off browned bits that have formed at the bottom of the pan.
- Add in the tomatoes, oregano powder, and ground pepper. Stir occasionally. Let the liquid from the tomatoes evaporate, might take about 5 minutes. Toss in the shrimps. Add in parsley. Cook for a few more minutes.
- Add in the zucchini noodles. Make sure that noodles are evenly coated.
- This recipe yields 4 servings.

Halibut with Cucumber Noodles in Coconut Curry

Ingredients:

For the noodles:

6 cups of cucumber noodles, spaghetti cut

3 tablespoons of olive oil

For the fish and broth:

2 tablespoons of olive oil

½ piece of an onion, finely chopped

2 teaspoons of curry powder

2 cups of chicken stock

½ cup of coconut milk

½ teaspoon of sea salt

4 pieces halibut fillet, skin removed

1/ cup chopped cilantro

2 tablespoons of lime juice

Procedure:

For the noodles:

- In a large non-stick pan, heat olive oil and cook cucumber noodles for about 5 minutes.

For the fish and broth:

- Heat olive oil in a large pot until it simmers, over olive oil.
- Add in onions and curry powder.
- Pour in the chicken stock.
- Add the coconut milk. Season with salt. Simmer.
- Coat the halibut with the sauce. Replace cover and let the halibut cooked for about 6 minutes.
- Remove the halibut from the broth. Set aside and transfer to a platter, cover with aluminum foil to keep it warm.
- Add cilantro and lime juice into the broth.
- Divide the noodles equally into 4 four small bowls. Gently pour over the broth. Place the halibut on top.
- This recipe serves a family of 4.

Smoked Salmon, Pasta and Dill

Ingredients:

4 cups of zucchini noodles (or yellow squash noodles), spiral cut

1 pack of smoked salmon (4 ounces), cut into thick strips

½ cup white wine

¼ cup of fresh dill, chopped

1 medium-sized red onion, minced

3 tablespoons of olive oil

1 pack of frozen peas (18 ounces), thawed and drained of liquid

1 lemon wedges

Procedure:

- Blanch and drain the noodles and place in a serving bowl.
- In a large pan, sauté onion in olive oil.
- Pour in white wine. Reduce the heat and simmer until sauce begins to thicken.

- Add in the peas, stirring gently.
- Simmer for a few minutes more before adding the salmon and dill.
- Simmer until sauce thickens some more.
- Pour the sauce over your zucchini noodles.
- Serve hot with lemon wedges.
- This makes 4 servings.

Crab Cakes in Lemon and Lime Aioli

Ingredients:

For the crab cakes:

2 medium-sized carrots, spaghetti noodle cut

1 pound crab meat

2 ½ tablespoons of garlic aioli

½ red bell pepper, minced

2 pieces scallions, minced

½ cu of almond meal

1 teaspoon of Old Bay seasoning

2 tablespoons of canola oil

For the aioli

1 cup garlic aioli

Lemon zest

Lime zest

Procedure:

- In a mixing bowl, put in carrot noodles, crab meat, aioli, scallions, red pepper, almond meal, and Old Bay seasoning. Make sure to mix well. Form and make 8 crab cakes. Chill in the refrigerator for about an hour.
- When chilled, take out of the ref and begin cooking.
- In a large non-stick pan, heat olive oil.
- Add in crab cakes one at a time. Brown both sides, that's about 3 t6 5 minutes for each side.
- In a small mixing bowl, prepare the aioli. Mix lemon zest and lime zest with garlic aioli.
- Serve your fried crab cakes with the homemade aioli.

Carrot Spaghetti with Smoked Salmon

This is dish is bursting with flavors. It is bursting with nutrients, too: Vitamin A, Vitamin C, and Omega-3 fatty acids.

Ingredients:

8 medium-sized carrots, spaghetti noodle cut

12 ounces of smoked salmon, chopped

4 scallions, minced

3 tablespoons of coconut oil

1 medium-sized red bell pepper, minced

4 cloves of garlic, minced

Juice and zest of 1 piece orange

½ teaspoons of stevia

½ teaspoon sriarcha

2 tablespoons of tamari, wheat-free (or you can use coconut aminos)

Procedure:

- In a skillet, heat coconut oil at medium to high heat.
- Add in the scallions and red bell pepper. Cook for about 5 minutes.
- Add garlic. When garlic aroma is released, you can add the orange zest and juice, stevia, tamari, and sriracha.
- Add in your carrot noodles and cook for about 5 minutes, stirring occasionally.
- Add in smoked salmon.
- Best served hot.
- Makes 4 servings.

Beef Stroganoff with Squash Ribbons

Ingredients:

For the noodles:

3 tablespoons low-fat butter

6 yellow squash, spiralized into ribbon noodles

For the beef stroganoff:

1 pound lean ground beef

2 cups beef stock

3 ounces of dried porcini mushrooms

8 ounces of crimini mushrooms, quartered

2 tablespoons butter

1 medium-sized onion, chopped

3 cloves of garlic, minced

½ cup white wine

1 teaspoon of dried thyme

½ teaspoon sea salt

¼ teaspoon ground black pepper

¼ cup arrowroot powder

2 tablespoons Worcestershire sauce

¼ cup sour cream

¼ cup chopped parsley

Procedure:

To prepare the noodles:

- Melt butter in a skillet set over medium to high heat. Add the yellow squash noodles and cook until "al dente".
- Set aside.

To prepare the beef stroganoff:

- The porcini mushrooms should be soaked in the beef stock about 3 hours prior to cooking.
- Take out the porcini mushrooms from the stock and slice. Set them aside. Save the beef stock as well.

- In a large pan, cook ground beef until golden brown. Remove from the frying pan and set aside.
- Melt butter in the pan. Add onions, porcini mushrooms, and crimini mushrooms. Cook for about 7 minutes or until vegetables are tender, with occasional stirring.
- Add garlic.
- Pour in the white wine. Scrape off those brown bits that may form at the bottom of the pan with a spoon.
- Put back the ground beef, and then add the seasonings.
- In a separate mixing bowl, whisk half a cup of the beef stock you reserved with arrowroot powder, and set aside.
- Add the remaining half of the beef stock into the pan. Add Worcestershire sauce. Add in the arrowroot and beef stock mixture. Simmer until it thickens.
- Add in the sour cream and chopped parsley, and simmer for about 2 to 3 minutes more.
- Pour the sauce over the squash noodles just before serving.
- This recipe serves 4.

Zucchini Spaghetti and Meatballs

Ingredients:

For the meatballs:

½ pound ground pork, lean

½ pound ground beef, lean

¼ cup of almond meal

2 egg yolks

6 tablespoons of olive oil, divided

1 medium-sized onion, finely chopped

1 clove of garlic, minced

½ teaspoon of dried thyme

½ teaspoon of ground black pepper

½ teaspoon of sea salt

¼ teaspoon of nutmeg

¼ teaspoon of allspice

2 cups of beef stock

1 cup of arrowroot powder

¼ cup non-fat cream

For the noodles:

6 medium-sized zucchini noodles, ribbon-cut

3 tablespoons of olive oil

Procedure:

How to prepare the meatballs:

- Heat a sauté pan over medium to high heat and add half of the olive oil.
- Add the onion, and when soft, you can add the garlic. Remove the pan from heat and allow the onions and garlic to cool down.
- In a separate mixing bowl, put the ground pork, ground beef, almond meal, the egg yolks, dried thyme, sea salt, ground black pepper, allspice, nutmeg, and the cooled onion and garlic. Mix thoroughly.
- Form the mixture into 1-inch meatballs.
- Heat the remaining half of the olive oil in a new skillet, set over medium to high heat.
- Fry the meatballs, making sure they are cooked all the way through, with constant stirring and flipping. Cooking

time can be 8 to 10 minutes. Remove from pan and set aside.

- On the safe pan, pour in 1 ½ of the beef stock. Scrape off the browned bits at the bottom of the pan, using a spoon.
- Adjust heat to medium and continue to simmer.
- In a separate mixing bowl, pour in the remaining ½ cup of the beef stock and whisk together with the arrowroot powder.
- Pour the beef stock and arrowroot mixture into the pan.
- Add the cream.
- Put back the cooked meatballs into the pan, making sure they are evenly coated with the cream sauce.

To prepare the noodles:

- Heat olive oil in a pan set over medium to high heat.
- Cook the zucchini noodles until tender; this may take about 5 minutes.
- This recipe makes 4 servings.

Do not overcrowd your pan when cooking the meatballs. Depending on the size of the pan that you are going to use, you might need to cook the meatballs in batches to make sure that they are evenly cooked.

Slow Cooked Pork with Apple Noodles

Ingredients:

For the pork

1 pound pork shoulder, cut into cubes

½ cabbage head, chopped

1 medium-sized red onion, chopped

1 fennel bulb, chopped

¼ cup of apple cider vinegar

1 cup beef stock

1 teaspoon of ground cinnamon

1 teaspoon of garlic powder

½ teaspoon of dried sage

1 teaspoon of sea salt

¼ teaspoon ground black pepper

For the noodles:

4 medium-sized apples, cored and stemmed, cut into wide flat noodles

3 tablespoons of olive oil

Procedure:

How to make the pork stew:

- Put all the ingredients in a 6-quart slow cooker.
- Put the lid on and cook over low heat for 8 to 10 hours.

How to make the apple noodles:

- In a skillet, heat olive oil.
- Cook apple noodles with constant stirring. Apples may be ready after 5 minutes.
- This recipe is good for 4 people.

You can substitute the apple noodles with zucchini if you want something lighter.

Chicken Biryani with Jicama Rice Noodles

This recipe is inspired by a popular rice dish from Northern China. While the typical biryani dish is layered and baked, this version is simpler because it is a one-pot meal.

Ingredients:

1 pound chicken breast fillet, skin removed, cut into 1-inch cubes

1 medium-sized jicama (Mexican yam), spiralized into thin spaghetti noodles

½ cup plain unflavored yogurt

2 tablespoons of curry powder

½ teaspoon of ground cinnamon

3 tablespoons of coconut oil

1 medium-sized onion, chopped

1 tablespoon of fresh ginger, grated

3 cloves of garlic, minced

½ cup chicken stock

3 tablespoons of fresh cilantro, chopped

Procedure:

- In a mixing bowl, put plain yogurt, cinnamon, and curry powder. Add in chicken pieces and evenly coat with the marinade. Cover and place inside the refrigerator for at least 3 hours.
- In a food processor, pulse the jicama until it bears a resemblance to rice. Set aside.
- Heat a large skillet over medium to high heat.
- Add in onion slices and cook for about 5 minutes.
- Add in the garlic and cook for about a minute.
- Put in the marinated chicken pieces (include the marinade), and cook for about 10 minutes or until chicken is cooked through. Don't forget to frequently turn to prevent the chicken from sticking to the pan.
- Gently pour in the chicken stock, and then add in the jicama rice noodles. Continue cooking until rice is soft, which may take about 5 minutes, with constant stirring.
- Add in the cilantro.
- This delectable recipe makes 4 people happy.

Cabbage Noodles with Ground Pork Stir-Fry

Ingredients:

1 pound ground pork

6 scallions, chopped

½ medium cabbage head, cut into fettuccine noodles (you can use green or red cabbage for this recipe)

1 medium-sized carrot, chopped

1 teaspoon of fresh ginger, grated

1 medium-sized red bell pepper, chopped

4 cloves of garlic, minced

2 tablespoons of rice vinegar

1 tablespoon of coconut aminos (or wheat-free tamari)

¼ teaspoon of chili oil

2 tablespoons of arrowroot powder

2 tablespoons of fresh orange juice

Procedure:

- In a large wok set to medium to high heat, cook ground pork until golden brown. This may take about 5 minutes. Remove pork from the pan and set aside.
- Remove pork fat if too much, and then put in the scallions, carrot, cabbage noodles, and red bell pepper. Cook, stirring occasionally, for about 5 minutes or until veggies are crisp-tender.
- Add in garlic and cook until you smell its aroma.
- Put back the cooked ground pork into the pan.
- In a separate mixing bowl, put the tamari, chili oil, rice vinegar, arrowroot powder, and orange juice extract.
- Add the sauce into the pan and cook for another 3 minutes or until sauce slightly thickens.
- Four people would be able to enjoy this recipe.

Ground Lamb in Carrot Noodles

Ingredients:

1 pound ground lamb

6 medium-sized carrot noodles, spaghetti cut

3 tablespoons of canola oil

1 teaspoon of ground cumin

½ teaspoon of ground cinnamon

1 teaspoon of ground coriander

1 medium-sized onion, chopped

3 cloves of garlic, chopped

3 tablespoons of fresh cilantro, chopped

Procedure:

- In a large skillet, cook ground lamb until golden brown. Remove from the pan and set aside.
- In the same skillet, add in canola oil and heat set to medium. Add in the cinnamon, cumin, coriander, and onion.

Cook for about 5 minutes with constant stirring.

- Add in the carrot noodles, cook until tender, which is about 5 minutes cooking time.
- Add in garlic and stir occasionally. Add in the cilantro.
- Makes 4 servings.

You can use the less expensive alternative to ground lamb, which could either be pork or beef.

Meat and Spaghetti Veggie Muffins

This homemade meat and veggie muffin recipe can be paired with your favorite spiralized salad dish.

Ingredients:

1 medium-sized zucchini noodles, spaghetti cut

1 medium-sized carrot noodles, spaghetti cut

½ pound ground beef

½ pound ground pork

½ onion, finely chopped

2 cloves of garlic, minced

1 teaspoon of dried thyme

1 tablespoon of Dijon mustard

1 tablespoon of Worcestershire sauce

1 teaspoon of homemade sriracha (or you can use store-bought)

1 medium-sized egg, lightly beaten

½ cup almond milk

½ cup almond meal

1 teaspoon sea salt

½ teaspoon ground black pepper

Procedure:

- Preheat your oven to 450°F.
- In a food processor or blender, pulse the zucchini and carrot noodles until they are like rice. You might need to do 20 1-second pulses.
- In a mixing bowl, transfer the zucchini and carrot rice. Add in the ground pork, ground beef, garlic, onion, beaten egg, mustard, Worcestershire sauce, almond meal, almond milk, sriracha, sea salt, and ground black pepper. Mix well.
- Fill your 12-muffin mold with the meatloaf mixture.
- Bake in the oven for about 20 minutes or until meatloaf is cooked.
- This is a recipe that can serve 4 people.

You may also omit ground pork, and just use ground beef if you like.

Beef Ragu with Potato Noodles

You can also substitute zucchini for the potatoes if you want a low-carb meal.

Ingredients:

4 cups of potato noodles, flat cut (you can also use zucchini or even squash)

1 ½ pounds ground beef (turkey meat is also a good alternative)

1 large yellow onion, chopped

3 large cloves of garlic, minced

1/3 cup of red wine

2 cans of Italian style diced tomatoes

1 large carrot, chopped

2 tablespoons of Italian seasoning

1/3 cup half and half

2 tablespoons of olive oil

Parmesan cheese, grated

Procedure:

- Heat a large skillet over medium to high heat. Add in the olive oil.
- Add the ground beef, onion, and garlic. Add in carrot. Cook for about 8 minutes or until ground beef turns brown.
- Pour in the red wine and cook for about 3 to 5 minutes. Stir constantly.
- When the wine evaporates, add in the canned tomatoes, do not drain.
- Next, add in the half and half and Italian seasoning.
- Reduce heat to medium. Simmer until the sauce thickens. This may take about 25 minutes.
- Pour the sauce over your noodles.
- Garnish with parmesan cheese. If you are on a strict Paleo Diet, skip the cheese.
- This recipe makes 4 servings.

Asian Inspired Zucchini Noodles and Pork in Peanut Sauce

Ingredients:

For the pork:

12 ounces pork tenderloin

1 teaspoon sesame oil

¼ cup of olive oil

½ teaspoon chili oil

¼ cup rice vinegar

2 tablespoons of coconut aminos (or wheat-free tamari)

2 tablespoons of coconut oil

For the noodles:

6 zucchini noodles, spaghetti cut

3 tablespoons coconut oil

¼ teaspoon chili oil

3 scallions, sliced

3 cloves of garlic, minced

1 cup nut butter sauce (see recipe at the end of the book)

2 tablespoons fresh cilantro, chopped

Procedure:

How to make pork:

- In a mixing bowl, combine sesame oil, chili oil, olive oil, rice vinegar, and tamari. Whisk until thoroughly mixed.
- Get a large zipper bag, place the pork and the marinade. Let it stand for at least 4 hours. Get more flavorful pork by marinating pork for 10 hours.
- Preheat oven to 425°F.
- In a large oven-safe pan, heat the coconut oil over medium to high heat.
- When the pork has been marinated enough, take out from the bag and pat dry using paper towels.
- Sear the pork tenderloin on all sides, allotting about 3 minutes for every side.
- Transfer to the oven roast for about 15 to 20 minutes (internal temperature is at 145°F).
- Once cooked, take out the tenderloin from the oven and let it rest for a 20 minutes covered with foil.

How to make the noodles:

- Heat coconut oil and chili oil in a skillet over medium to high heat.
- Add the zucchini noodles, scallions, and ginger. Cook until zucchini is tender.
- Add garlic.
- Add in the nut butter sauce, cook for another 1 minute.
- Add in the cilantro.
- Serve noodles topped with the roasted pork tenderloin.
- This recipe makes 4 servings.

Classic Meaty Pizza and Pasta

Ingredients:

For the pasta:

4 zucchini noodles, fettuccine cut

Sea salt

For the marina sauce:

2 cans of crushed tomatoes, do not drain

2 tablespoons of olive oil

4 cloves of garlic, finely minced

1 shallot, finely minced

1 tablespoon dried basil

1 tablespoon dried oregano

1/8 teaspoon red pepper flakes, crushed

½ teaspoon sea salt

¼ teaspoon ground black pepper

For the pizza pasta

4 ounces bacon, sliced

4 ounces Italian sausage, browned and crumbled

4 ounces pepperoni

4 ounces Genoa salami

6 ounces mozzarella cheese, grated

2 ounces parmesan cheese, grated

Procedure:

To make pasta:

- Place the zucchini noodles in a large colander.
- Add salt and let it sit for about 30 minutes.
- Rinse and pat dry with paper towels.

To make the marinara sauce:

- Heat olive oil in a pan over medium to high heat.
- Add shallots and then add the garlic.
- Add tomatoes, oregano, basic, red pepper flakes, sea salt, and ground black pepper. Simmer over medium to low heat to thicken the sauce.

To make the pizza and pasta

- Preheat oven to 375°F.
- In a mixing bowl, mix zucchini noodles, marinara sauce, bacon, sausage, salami, and pepperoni.
- Transfer to a 9x9 inch baking pan.
- Sprinkle with mozzarella cheese and parmesan cheese on top.
- Bake for about 20 minutes.

Fettuccine Alfredo

Ingredients:

For the pasta:

6 zucchini fettuccine cut noodles

3 tablespoons of olive oil

Sea salt

For the sauce:

8 ounces cream cheese

¼ cup heavy cream

¼ cup unsalted butter

½ cup Asiago cheese, grated

Procedure:

How to make the pasta:

- Put the zucchini noodles in a colander and add salt
- Let it sit there for 30 minutes before rinsing. Pat with paper towels to dry.

- Heat olive oil in a large pan over medium to high heat.
- Cook zucchini noodles for about 5 minutes. Set aside.

How to make the sauce:

- In a sauce pan, place all the ingredients and simmer over medium heat.
- When the cheese melts and the sauce thickens, remove from heat and top over zucchini noodles.
- Serves 4.

Classic Pesto Spaghetti

Ingredients:

For the pasta:

6 zucchini spaghetti cut noodles

3 tablespoons olive oil

Sea salt

For the pesto sauce:

2 cups fresh basil leaves

3 cloves of garlic

¼ cup of pine nuts

½ cup extra virgin olive oil

½ cup parmesan cheese

½ teaspoon of sea salt

¼ teaspoon of ground black pepper

Procedure:

How to make the pasta:

- Sprinkle salt over the zucchini noodles and let it sit for 30 minutes. Give a quick rinse.
- Heat olive oil in a skillet over medium to high heat.
- Cook noodles "al dente".

How to make the pesto sauce:

- In a food processor or blender, put all the ingredients for the pesto sauce and process for about 20 seconds.
- Serve over the zucchini pasta.
- This recipe makes 4 servings.

Carrot Macaroni and Cheese

Ingredients:

6 medium-sized carrots, elbow-shaped cut

2 tablespoons of canola oil

¼ cup butter

½ cup heavy cream

8 ounces of cream cheese, cubed

3 ounces of cheddar cheese, grated

½ teaspoon of sea salt

¼ teaspoon of ground black pepper

Procedure:

- Heat canola oil in a skillet over medium to high heat.
- Add carrots and cook "al dente". Remove from heat and set aside.
- In another sauce pan, melt butter.
- Add in the heavy cream and the cream cheese. Reduce heat to medium, with occasional stirring.

- Add in the cheddar cheese and simmer until cheese has melted and sauce thickens.
- Add in sea salt and pepper.
- Throw in carrot noodles. Mix well.
- This recipe is good for 4 people.

Classic Chow Mein Dish

Ingredients:

1 pound ground pork

6 carrots, spaghetti cut

6 scallions, sliced

1 tablespoon of fresh ginger, grated

1 can water chestnuts, drained, sliced

6 ounces shitake mushrooms, sliced

3 cloves of garlic, minced

½ cup chicken stock

2 tablespoons of arrowroot powder

2 tablespoons coconut aminos (or wheat-free tamari)

½ teaspoon sriracha sauce

Procedure:

- Cook ground pork in a skillet until golden brown. Remove from heat and side aside.

- Using the pork fat, cook the shitake mushrooms, scallions, water chestnuts, and ginger until soft.
- Add in the carrot noodles and cook for 5 minutes.
- Add in garlic, before putting back the ground pork into the skillet.
- In a separate mixing bowl, mix chicken broth, tamari, sriracha, and arrowroot powder.
- Pour in the mixed sauce to the skillet. Simmer until sauce thickens.
- This can serve 4 people.

Crispy Apple Dessert

Ingredients:

6 large apples, cored but do not peel, flat cut

1/3 cup of almond flour

½ cup pecans, chopped

1/3 cup whole oats (do not use instant oats)

3 tablespoons brown sugar

½ stick of butter

1 ½ teaspoon cinnamon

½ teaspoon fresh ginger

Juice from 1 lemon

Procedure:

- Preheat your oven to 375°F.
- In a mixing bowl, put the apples. Add in 1 teaspoon cinnamon.

- Add the ginger, brown sugar, and lemon juice. Mix well until apples are evenly coated.
- In a separate mixing bowl, mix almond flour, pecans, oats, brown sugar, and the remaining ½ teaspoon of cinnamon. Mix them thoroughly with a fork. You need to get a crumbly texture.
- Arrange the apples into a 10-inch pie pan. Cover with the "crumbly topping".
- Bake in the oven for an hour or until the filling is hot and the top is crispy and caramelized a little.
- Remove from the oven. Let it stand for about 5 minutes.
- This recipe can feed 6 to 8 individuals.

Sweet Potato with Pecans Pudding

Ingredients:

1 pound sweet potatoes, flat or julienned cut

3 medium-sized eggs, beaten

2 tablespoons unsalted melted butter

2 cups non-fat milk

½ cup raisins, plumped in how water, drained

¼ cup pecan halves

½ cup of maple syrup

1 teaspoon cinnamon

Procedure:

- Preheat your oven to 325°F.
- Brush an 8x8 inch pan with butter or non-stick cooking spray.
- In a bowl, combine all the ingredients before pouring into the baking pan.
- Bake for 1 hour.

- This recipe is good for 6 to 8 people.

Baked Apple

Ingredients:

4 apples, cored, stemmed, cut into thin ribbons

3 medium-sized eggs

3 tablespoons coconut oil

½ teaspoon stevia

½ cup orange juice

1 cup almond meal flour

¼ cup tapioca flour

1 ½ teaspoons cinnamon

¼ teaspoon sea salt

1 teaspoon vanilla extract

Procedure:

- Preheat your oven to 350°F.
- Brush a 9x13 inch pan with coconut oil.
- In a mixing bowl, beat the eggs.
- Add in ½ cup coconut oil, orange juice, stevia, tapioca flour, ¾ cup almond

meal, 1 teaspoon cinnamon, vanilla extract, and sea salt.

- Mix in the apple noodles.
- In another mixing bowl, combine the remaining ¼ cup almond meal with half a teaspoon cinnamon and 2 tablespoons of melted coconut oil. Sprinkle this mixture over the apple krugel.
- Bake in the oven for about an hour.
- This recipe serves 8.

Crispy Pear

Ingredients:

4 pears, fettuccine cut

½ teaspoon stevia

½ teaspoon lemon zest

1 teaspoon lemon juice

½ teaspoon sea salt

2 teaspoons ground cinnamon

½ teaspoon ground ginger

¾ cup walnuts, chopped

¼ cup coconut flakes

¼ cup almond meal

¼ cup coconut oil, melted

Procedure:

- Preheat your oven to 350°F.
- In mixing bowl, put pear noodles, stevia, lemon zest and juice, ginger, ¼ teaspoon of the sea salt, and 1 teaspoon of the cinnamon.

- Brush a 9x9 inch baking pan with butter or oil. Pour the mixture in.
- In another bowl, put the chopped walnuts, almond meal, coconut flakes, coconut oil, remaining sea salt, and the remaining cinnamon. Mix thoroughly.
- Sprinkle over the pear noodle mixture.
- Bake for about 45 minutes.
- This dessert is good for 4 people.

Carrot Muffins

Ingredients:

3 medium-sized carrots, spaghetti cut

2 pieces ripe bananas, mashed

½ teaspoon baking powder

½ teaspoon baking soda

1 ¼ cup almond meal

¼ teaspoon stevia

¼ teaspoon sea salt

1 tablespoon ground cinnamon

1 teaspoon ground ginger

4 medium-sized eggs, beaten

¼ cup coconut oil, melted

¼ cup coconut milk

1 teaspoon vanilla extract

Procedure:

- Preheat your oven to 350°F.

- Line with parchment papers a 12-piece muffin cups or tray.
- In a mixing bowl, sift almond meal, stevia, baking powder, baking soda, cinnamon, ginger, and sea salt.
- In a separate mixing bowl, whisk bananas, coconut oil, coconut milk, eggs, and vanilla extract.
- Fold the wet ingredients with the dry ingredients, mixing thoroughly.
- Add in the carrot noodles.
- Pour into the muffin cups.
- Bake for about 25 minutes.
- Let the muffins cool before serving.

Lemon Custard with Pear

Ingredients:

Custard:

3 medium-sized eggs, lightly beaten

3 cups coconut milk

½ teaspoon stevia

1 teaspoon vanilla extract

1 tablespoon lemon zest

Pear:

2 pieces pears, stemmed, cut into spaghetti noodles

1 teaspoon ground cinnamon

¼ teaspoon stevia

½ teaspoon ground anise

Procedure:

To make custard:

- Preheat your oven to 300°F.
- Fill half full with boiling water a 9x13 inch baking pan. Put in the oven.
- In a mixing bowl, combine stevia, eggs, coconut milk, lemon zest, and vanilla extract. Whisk to mix all the ingredients well.
- Pour the mixture into six ramekins and place in the hot water bath. Put back in the oven.
- Bake for about 75 to 90 minutes.
- Cool the custard for at least an hour before putting inside the refrigerator.

Make the pears:

- Put pear noodles, cinnamon, stevia, and anise into a mixing bowl and mix well.
- Place the pear noodles on top of the custard before serving.
- This recipe serves 6.

Chapter 15 Kitchen Staples

Sriracha Recipe

Ingredients:

1 ½ pound spicy red chili peppers, stemmed, de-seeded, chopped

½ cup apple cider vinegar

¼ cup tomato paste

10 cloves of garlic, finely minced

1 tablespoon of coconut aminos (or whole wheat tamari)

½ teaspoon stevia

1 teaspoon sea salt

Procedure:

- In a food processor or blender, mix and puree all the ingredients until you get a smooth consistency.
- In a separate sauce pan, simmer the puree over medium to high heat, stirring occasionally until thick.

- Store in a sterilized container and refrigerate. This can stay fresh for a month.

Garlic Aioli

Ingredients:

2 cloves of garlic, minced

2 egg yolks

2 tablespoons of red wine vinegar

¼ teaspoon sea salt

½ teaspoon Dijon mustard

1 ½ cups extra virgin olive oil

Procedure:

- In a food processor bowl, put garlic, vinegar, mustard, salt, and egg yolks.
- Turn on the processor.
- Working through the sprout opening, add the extra virgin coconut oil, drop by drop, until you have about 20 drops. Then add the oil in a thin stream until the mixture emulsifies.
- You can keep this aioli in the refrigerator for up to a week.

Conclusion

Thank you again for buying this book!

I hope this book was able to help you create mouth-watering vegetable dishes with the aid of a spiralizer, a kitchen device that will improve the way you prepare nutrient-dense dishes such as soups, pasta, rice, noodles, salads and stir-fries.

Moreover, I hope this book was able to inspire you to eat more organic produce not only because of its clean flavors but because plant-based meals provide us with numerous health benefits such as glowing skin, healthier bones, faster metabolism and lowered risk of having infections and disease.

The next step is to spend more time in the kitchen and discover ways to incorporate spiralized vegetables into your daily meals. Your family will definitely appreciate the amazing flavors, textures and nutrients of spiralized dishes. Who knows, they may even be convinced to adopt a vegetable-based diet for the rest of their lives.

Finally, if you enjoyed this book, please take the time to share your thoughts and post a review on Amazon. It'd be greatly appreciated!

Thank you and good luck!

Made in the USA
San Bernardino, CA
03 December 2015